$\mathcal{K}$'s Kitchen

Five Generation Legacy Of Family Favorites

by

"$\mathcal{K}$"

Carolyn Murdock Moore
Author

First Grade
Kosciusko, Mississippi

Published by Carolyn Murdock Moore
Co-published/Edited by Charles Raburn Moore

Front Cover Conceptual Design by Carolyn Murdock Moore
Back Cover Design by Charles Raburn Moore

Cover Art by Wanta
Artistic Perceptions
Augusta, Georgia

Library of Congress Control Number 2001126601

ISBN: 0-9710907-0-X

WIMMER
COOKBOOKS

ConsolidatedGraphics

1-800-548-2537

Dedications...

To Dutch, my husband of forty years—a stable marriage that's been like a ride to the Rocky Mountains in a wagon drawn by horses. Dutch is jack-of-all-trades and master of a few—his main occupation has been an operating engineer of heavy equipment for forty-seven years.

To Charles R. and H. Ronald Moore, my sons. I've always loved you unconditionally. When I do for one, I do equally for the other. I love you yesterday, today and forever.

To Kristen Nicole and Karla LaRae, my lovely granddaughters. You've brightened my life in many ways. I'm honored to be your grandparent—"*K-K*"

To Dr. John G. Downer of Lexington, Mississippi—my family doctor and family friend of thirty-two years. I've made his sweet potato chess pies since 1980. John says they are the best in the whole wide world. He loves cooking Italian and soul foods. I highly value his opinions concerning my health and greatly admire his sense of humor.

In Honor Of...

The Leaders—my sister Elsie, her husband Douglas and their son Donald of Aiken, South Carolina.

I have always thought of Doug Leader more as a brother by birth than a brother-in-law. Early in his marriage to my sister, Doug told me, "If you ever need me I am only a phone call away." He's been a faithful confidant to my family and me for forty-eight years. Doug and Elsie are continually blessed for their many acts of good deeds for this family as well as for others and have set a wonderful example of humanity for others to emulate.

The Kerleys—my niece Barbara Leader Kerley, her husband Bill and their children Rachel and Cameron of Aiken, South Carolina.

The Martins—my sister Margaret Murdock and her husband Hardy of Moss Point, Mississippi, their son, Murdock Martin and wife Susan Crawford of Washington, DC, and their son, Edward Martin, his wife Lisa and their children Taylor Elizabeth and Jeffrey of Lufkin, Texas.

In Memory Of...

My Brothers
James Clinton Murdock and Hugh McMillan Murdock

My Parents
James Howard and Fannie Meek "Herring" Murdock

My Paternal Grandparents
Hugh McMillan and Margaret "Starr" Murdock

My Maternal Grandparents
Isaac Abner and Minnie Leola "Herring" Herring

My Paternal Great Grandparents
James and Hannah Elizer "Ayers" Starr

My Maternal Great Grandparents
Dr. Isaac Arnold and Susan Caroline "Meek" Herring

My Maternal Great Grandparents
John Russell and Bell "Farris" Herring

My Paternal Great Aunt
Mary Murdock

Our Family Friend
Florence Price

Acknowledgments...

Thank you Lord for giving me the gift of cooking, the strength, knowledge, and guidance to pen this cookbook. Without Thee, it would have been impossible.

A special thanks to my sons Charles and H. Ronald, for being my honest critics, rating my recipes on a scale of 1 – 10 and forcing me to improve until a high rating was achieved.

Thanks to Dutch, my husband of forty years, for his patience. I can always light up his eyes and see a special smile when I cook his favorite foods. I love you.

Thanks to Charles for his untiring efforts as my editor and co-publisher.

Introduction...
Getting to know the author

Carolyn Murdock was born on the heels of the great depression of the 1930s in Attala County, Mississippi. Carolyn's birthplace, Kosciusko, is widely known as TV talk show host Oprah Winfrey's family's hometown. Carolyn began cooking when she was 7 years old—preparing complete meals for her family of six on the old wood stove by the time she was 11. She received her nickname of "*K*" from a nephew who struggled to say "Aunt Carolyn". Aunt K, as she was affectionately known from that time forward later dropped the "Aunt" portion. The name "*K*" stuck.

In the mid 1950s, Carolyn moved to Springfield, South Carolina with her parents so her father could work on the Savannah River Project. She became a standout basketball player at Springfield High School—one night tossing in 44 points in little more than half a game. She later graduated from Springfield High School with the Class of '57. She has wonderful memories living her teenage years in this hospitable small town and continues to keep in touch with friends.

Following high school, Carolyn returned to Mississippi and became employed in management with Millner Enterprises at the famous King Edward Hotel in Jackson. The King Edward was known as home for the Mississippi State Legislature while in session—a gathering place for governors, congressmen, movie stars, and oilmen to conduct business and to serve as headquarters for conventions of all types. She has expressed that it was a pleasure to have worked for this establishment. Carolyn also sidelined as a freelance model until she married Dutch Moore of Lexington, Mississippi. She then abandoned her career aspirations to be a full-time wife and mother. She has said that being a mother has been the central theme and highlight of her life. Carolyn and her husband Dutch relocated to Lexington to raise their two children, Charles and Hugh Ronald. During the sixteen years in Lexington, she worked in childcare so she could meet the challenges of parenthood. Later, she managed the local newspaper route for Clarion-Ledger Jackson Daily News, the state newspaper. Being a housewife much of the time allowed Carolyn, a.k.a. "*K*", to pursue her other aspiration—cooking.

$\mathcal{K}$ returned to Kosciusko to care for her ailing father after the death of her mother in 1982. During the mid 1980s, $\mathcal{K}$ developed, marketed, and promoted her pancake syrup. $\mathcal{K}$ and Dutch attended the graduation of their oldest son Charles at Mississippi State University in 1986. In 1992, they witnessed their son Ronald graduate from Nashville Auto Diesel College.

Precipitated by the death of her father, $\mathcal{K}$ and Dutch packed up and moved to Bath, South Carolina in the mid '90s to be closer to their two sons now located in the Augusta, Georgia area. In case you are wondering where Bath, South Carolina is on the map—it is located between Augusta, Georgia and Aiken, South Carolina on Highway 421 in an area known as "The Valley". In 2001, they were proud to see Ronald receive a second diploma—this time in Environmental Horticulture from Augusta Technical College in Augusta, Georgia.

And just what does $\mathcal{K}$ do when she is not cooking? She is an avid gardener—especially of the exotic Angel's Trumpets. She performs the "Dances of the Century" in formal wear for special occasions. Her other hobbies include family fellowship, playing card games and dominoes, designing clothes, gardening (flowers and vegetables), developing recipes, making crafts, designing costume jewelry, interior decorating, photography, meeting the public, and helping to "make someone's day".

In 1985, her sons asked her to do a cookbook—with everything she had developed from scratch plus other delectable recipes from family and friends dating back into the 1800s. She bought empty recipe books to contain the recipes, but the books lay dormant until January 2001...

As with all things, the times and conditions have changed over the years for those of us who cook. Today, we take for granted that we cook with gas or electric heat, shop in luxurious supermarkets, store our food in refrigerators and freezers, and warm the leftovers in a microwave oven. However, life was not as easy in those early days. Before Mom could cook on the family stove, my grandfather or uncle had to "fetch" the wood about an hour beforehand and stoke "Old Woody". Once lit, Woody would be ready for cooking in about a half hour. Because of the rural country lifestyle in post-depression Mississippi, Mom's family did not have modern electric appliances such as microwave ovens, mixers, and blenders. Food preparation was difficult at best.

Since the days of her childhood, Mom has regularly cooked for her ever-expanding family—with electricity and natural gas. We who have enjoyed her cooking over the years can authenticate its excellence—and most of us carry more with us than just the memories. This cookbook is made available to you by the request of my brother and I to leave a legacy of Mom's kitchen knowledge, favorite recipes and tasty dishes. Welcome to *K's Kitchen Secrets*.

P. S. – Mom would LOVE to hear from you about her cookbook. Please direct all correspondence to:

K's Kitchen Secrets
P. O. Box 1354
Bath, SC 29816
(803) 593-2570

– Charles

Kosciusko, Mississippi...
Attala County History

Kosciusko, Mississippi... my native hometown is located in the central part of Mississippi. It was named for a famous Polish general who faithfully served on General George Washington's staff during the Revolutionary War. Thaddeus Kosciuszko was born in Poland. The military academy at West Point is a tribute to his military excellence and serves as his continuing contribution to us. One of the most revealing feats of Kosciuszko is the rock garden still enjoyed on the grounds of the United States Military Academy at West Point. Thaddeus Kosciuszko was well represented in my high school history book.

Attala County gets it's name from an Indian Princess named Atala who was the brainchild of Chateaubriand, a Frenchman. Francois-Rene de Chataubriand was born in Saint-Malo, France in 1768. During his life he sailed to America gathering information and later writing *Atala*, the story a blend of naturalism and religion. This book was well received by book lovers who were eager for stories of America. The make-believe princess made her debut in *Atala*, giving her name to my home county.

Secrets on the Eve of Christmas

Secrets talked and secrets bought
On the eve of Christmas . . .
Mom selects them at the store
Wrapped and tied in tin foil galore!

Sister plunders in disguise,
For the whispers make her wise.
She's expecting a big surprise
On the eve of Christmas.

Secrets here and secrets there
On the eve of Christmas . . .

Brother comes in from a date,
Eating iced cake from a crystal plate.
Heeds the chimes of silver bells
As the bubbling of tree lights swells.

With glistening ice cycles, with angel hair
That gleams toward the star that bids greetings
To homecoming children around the cheery fire
That sparkles and crackles with Christmas delight for Mom and Dad.

Mistletoe with red holly berries
Decorate the halls where secret treasures are stored
Lend bliss with red bells dangling
As chimes ring out "Bless be the tie that binds"
Our hearts in love, at home with God at Christmas time.

The crackle of brown paper breaks silence
To secrets here and secrets there impart.
Now a waltz toward the piano that starts
Carol singing, spirited hearts melt the atmosphere with,
"I'm glad it's Christmas in my old home in nineteen and fifty-three!"

By my mother Fannie Meek Herring Murdock
"Grandma"

(Christmas, 1953 in Springfield, South Carolina)

Reliving Memories...
While Penning

While you may be thinking about cooking up your favorite dish, I relived these memories of the olden days while penning this cookbook. I am thinking about how hard it would be to go back in time after using all the modern conveniences that we have today. Think about it...no cars! People used horses, wagons, carriages, horse and buggy or personal hoof to visit or take care of errands.

We washed clothes in a large black wash pot with plenty of firewood beneath. When the clothes were put into the boiling water, lye soap was used to scrub the clothes clean (lye is a strong alkaline substance used as a cleaning solution). After plunging the clothes with a handle, we'd remove the clothes with the handle to three tubs of rinse water and then through a homemade tub of starch and water. Then we hung the clothes out to dry. We usually washed clothes once or twice a week. Then we'd iron them by using a smoothing iron with handles that had either been heated on the stove or in the fireplace over coals. The irons were made smooth on the ironing surface by using cedar leaves or a wax process. Smoothing would make the irons glide easily over the dampened clothes.

There was no electricity and no electric irons. The people used coal oil lamps to see at nighttime—many types and designs. Many, for nighttime riding in the horse and buggy, used a lantern. There was a special place on the buggy to hold the lantern. Nightriders and messengers used a torch.

Having running water in the homes was unheard of in the early 1900s. One had to dig wells many feet deep until a good vein of water was found, installing curbing to line the well. Other people were fortunate enough to have natural springs or ever flowing artesian wells—good water forced up by underground pressure. Springs and artesian wells usually contain many minerals in the water. It was my belief that this type of well was a godsend.

A pot of turnip greens or collards with a fresh skillet of cornbread should be savored, relished and otherwise appreciated by its partakers, right down to the last cup of pot liquor. Just think what it would be like today to go to the garden, pick the vegetables, come to the house and prepare the vegetables for cooking, fire up the wood stove then cook lunch—one meat, three vegetables, a salad, cornbread, iced tea and a desert. This would take all morning to prepare, but only forty-five minutes for a family to consume. And then there were the mountains of pots, pans and dishes to wash.

When I was kid in school, my mother often prepared these types of meals for us. I would come in from school and clean the kitchen from lunch so it would be clean enough to prepare dinner. I promised myself that I would be faithful to do three things when I had a family of my own: First, I would always wash my dishes *as* I cooked, never leaving my kitchen after meals until all is cleaned. Second, my beds would never go unmade and third, my family clothes would never stack up on me. To this day I can count on my fingers how many times these three things have gone undone. It is my belief that a person's home tells you a lot about a person. To me, it's quite a pleasure coming into a tidy home, but a dread when dishes are not done, beds are unmade, loads of dirty clothes wait to be done, and the floors need to be cleaned. An unkempt house elevates my stress level—enough to make me want to leave home and never look back.

While penning this cookbook I'm tending a garden, taking care of my yard of flowers and letting a few things slide until I'm finished. But I'm never letting my promises go undone. I've had people ask me how do you leave your home? On this I reply, "You be the judge! I can say, "It looks as well as I do!"

I've denoted recipes in this cookbook that I developed (or doctored) with a superscript $\mathcal{K}$ in the title. I've designated my personal comments about a recipe in *italics*.

Substitutions of Ingredients

1 teaspoon baking powder = ¼ teaspoon baking soda plus ½ teaspoon cream of tarter

1 cup buttermilk = 1 cup 4% milk into which 1 tablespoon vinegar or lemon juice has been added and stirred. Let stand for 5 minutes before using.

1 square chocolate (1 ounce) = 4 tablespoons cocoa plus ½ tablespoon of butter

1 tablespoon corn starch (a thickening agent) = 2 tablespoons flour

1 teaspoon dried herbs = 1 tablespoon fresh herbs

1 tablespoon prepared mustard = 1 teaspoon dry mustard

1/8 teaspoon garlic powder = 1 small clove of crushed garlic

3 small bananas = 1 cup mashed bananas

1 cup milk = ½ cup evaporated milk plus ½ cup water

OVEN CHARTS

Very Slow Oven	250° to 300° F
Slow Oven	300° to 325° F
Moderate Oven	325° to 375° F
Medium Hot Oven	375° to 400° F
Hot Oven	400° to 450° F
Very Hot Oven	450° to 500° F
Broil	Over 500° F

All temperatures in this cookbook are in degrees Fahrenheit (° F) and all times and temperatures are for sea level. Adjustments must be made for baking at elevations significantly different than sea level. Also, different ovens cook foods at different rates—so it is best to know your oven! I prefer to use a conventional electric or gas oven.

Standard Terms In Cooking

Weights – Measures – Equivalents

3 teaspoons = 1 tablespoon
1 tablespoon = ½ fluid ounce (oz.)
4 tablespoons = ¼ cup
8 tablespoons = ½ cup
12 tablespoons = ¾ cup
16 tablespoons = 1 cup
5 1/3 tablespoons = 1/3 cup
10 2/3 tablespoons = 2/3 cup
1 cup = 8 fluid ounces
1 cup = ½ pint
2 cups = 1 pint
4 cups = 1 quart
2 pints = 1 quart
4 quarts = 1 gallon
8 quarts = 1 peck
4 pecks = 1 bushel
1 ounce (oz.) = 2 tablespoons liquid
16 ounces = 1 pound
1 jigger = 3 tablespoon (1 ½ oz.)
Dash (dry) = less than 1/8 teaspoon
Dash (liquid) = few drops
Butter, margarine, or oleo, 1 stick = ½ cup
Flour, 1 pound, plain (all purpose) = 4 cups, sifted
Sugar, 1 pound brown = 2 ¼ to 2 ½ cups
Sugar, 1 pound granulated = 2 ¼ cups
Sugar, 1 pound powdered = 3 ½ to 4 cups, sifted

Long ago, cooks did not have standard-sized spoons, cups, bowl, etc. The cooks used commonly available items when measuring out their ingredients. For example, many recipes called for heaps of flour or heaps of sugar. A heap was defined as the amount of sugar or flour that could be scooped out of a barrel or flour sack with the person's cupped hand. Another recipe called for a thimble or pinch of soda, salt, etc. Another called for a tinge or a smidgeon of spice. Lard was measured in units of hen eggs. Even without accurate means for measuring the ingredients, much of the best food I've ever eaten was made with these crude techniques. I still use similar methods for measuring today when cooking certain foods. Maybe you will find a few in my book.

K's Cooking Definitions

Baste: To repeatedly spoon or brush food as it cooks with melted butter or liquid. Keeps food from drying out. Frequently used in BBQ, grilling or oven-baked poultry.

Beat: To stir rapidly in a circular motion.

Boned: To have removed all of bones from meat.

Butter: Churned milk fat or solidified vegetable fat. In this cookbook, many recipes specify butter. This means that you make the choice about richness of the food you are preparing. For more richness (and cholesterol) add real butter from the churned cow's milk. For most cooking needs, however, I recommend the use of vegetable margarine or shortening. Never use whipped butter or margarine when making any cake in this book. One stick of butter is the same as 1/2 cup of butter or shortening.

Coating: To cover such as coating meat with seasoned flour prior to frying. This is frequently done in a brown bag or small bowl. It is best to drain or dry meat well before coating and shake off excess before frying.

Core: To remove the center of a fruit or vegetable.

Dunk: To immerse, poke under, to dip and eat.

Fold: A process used to gently combine a light, airy mixture such as beaten eggs or egg whites with a heavier mixture. This consists of a motion of down, across, up and over. This gently turns the mixture over and over combining the ingredients.

Heaping: Means all the measuring utensil will hold—"rounded and then some" as Pappy Murdock would say.

Lard: Pork fat from hogs that has been cooked out; used in making biscuits, cakes, and frying. Lard was used exclusively in olden days. Due to lard being high in cholesterol it is not as popular today.

Mince:	To cut foods or herbs into extremely small pieces.
Mix:	Combine ingredients by use of an electric mixer or spoon.
Omit:	To leave out of a recipe; or fail to include.
Optional:	Your choice of whether to use or not to use in a recipe.
Prick:	To place small holes in surface of food. For an unbaked piecrust insert the tines of a fork all over so that it bakes without rising. This lets the air escape from under the crust as it bakes.
Sift:	To pass dry ingredients together through a fine mesh sifter (screen) in order for large pieces of ingredients to be removed. Makes ingredients lighter and more uniform.
Simmer:	To cook food gently in liquid at a temperature just high enough that tiny bubbles break the surface.
Tenderized:	Tenderizing meat mechanically is accomplished by breaking down tough fibers through pounding. Meat markets use a machine to tenderize—this is usually done free of charge. Round steak is great when tenderized, coated and fried.
Toast:	To brown in an oven on low heat (pecans for example).
Tongs:	A kitchen cooking utensil consisting of two long, hinged arms used for grabbing, holding and lifting foods.
Well:	A hole made in the middle of ingredients such as flour mixture—typically used for biscuits, cornbread, hushpuppies, etc.
Whip:	To beat ingredients rapidly such that air is entrapped in the mixture and the mixture expands in volume and homogeneity. This is typically done for egg whites when making meringue, whipped cream or cakes. The resulting mixture will be light and fluffy.

K's Helpful Hints and Kitchen Secrets

1. I've included many helpful hints and secrets in my recipes. I believe the following hints and secrets will be very useful in accomplishing desired texture, taste and satisfaction in your cooking endeavors.

2. It is of utmost importance when you are using a new recipe to read and understand the recipe. Find out what ingredients are required, understand the procedure and temperatures you will be using, the size of mixing bowls and skillets or baking pans.

3. Moist, light and fine textured cakes are accomplished by having all ingredients at room temperature, beating the butter and sugar until light and fluffy, adding eggs one at a time and beating the hell out of the mixture after each addition. Finally, add half the dry ingredients initially and then the other half in the final stages. Beat the total mixture well for about a minute after all ingredients are added.

4. To remove air from pound cakes after batter has been placed into baking pans and before putting into the oven, hold each side of cake pan and bang the pan on the floor hard 3 or 4 times. This allows the air to dissipate from the batter.

5. After cooking the pie filling, beat the cooked pie filling with an electric mixer on high for 30 seconds to make the pie filling fluffy. This will eliminate lumps, if any.

6. To toast pecans in oven, place pecans on large pie tin and bake in oven for 20 minutes at 200° F. Turn over frequently. This procedure allows the pecans to dry out and they will be crunchy. I use this technique when making pecan pies and salads, etc.

7. I never use whipped margarine to make cakes. Only use whipped margarine if specifically stated in the recipe. Whenever butter is specified in a recipe, you may use unwhipped vegetable margarine or shortening. The margarine or shortening can be either store brand or brand name, but not whipped. This is very important.

8. Always use a good quality brand of plain (all-purpose) or self-rising flour. Sift flour before using only if the flour is lumpy. Typically, if a recipe calls for sifted flour, measure and sift all the dry ingredients together to remove any lumps and to incorporate the ingredients.

9. In measuring ingredients for a cake, always use the same-sized measuring cup. If three different size cups are used, your proportions will not be balanced, therefore your recipe most likely will not work and you'll be disappointed.

10. It is best not to cut a hot cake until it is cool. You'll lose moisture. It's hard in my home to keep my husband from cutting into a hot pound cake. He's ready to get the butter and have a feast. If he does get into the hot cake before I want him to, I replace the wedge-shaped hole with waxed paper or foil to preserve the moisture. Any cake made with real butter or sour cream is best if it is not cut for three days. The cake is moist and flavor enhanced.

11. To remove a cake from a cake pan upside right (example a pound cake), place a plate over the cake pan. Using potholders and with both hands, hold each side of plate and pan, and turn over rapidly. Place another plate over the cake, sandwiching the cake between the two plates. Then turn over again. Cake will be up side right. This may be adventurous the first few times you try this! But the more you do this procedure, the easier it gets.

12. To boil eggs always start in cold water (helps to prevent cracking while boiling). When eggs are done (boiled 8 to 12 minutes) pour off hot water from the pot toss eggs up and down to lightly break the shells. Add cold water just to cover. Peel when ready to use or eat.

13. When cooking vegetables use the least amount of water so your vegetables have more flavor and less juice. When finished you'll have the full flavor of the vegetables. When too much water is added you loose your valuable nutrients down the drain in the excess water.

14. When peeling onions, wear rubber gloves and hold each onion under cold running water. This helps to prevent the juice from getting in your eyes. If onion juice happens to get into your eyes, rinse them with cold water and look at a dark green color for 2 minutes.

15. When using a powdered sugar base for cake icing and you want an easy design, use a piece of oiled crisscross plastic basket weave and press (roll) into icing. Repeat until all sides are completed. Some wedding cake decorators use this method. This crisscross plastic weave can come from a laundry basket.

16. Clothespins are very useful in the kitchen. I use them to keep my cereals, flour, corn meal, and crackers closed. Helps prevent moisture and critters from creeping in.

17. Use this idea at your own risk. When chopping pecans place them in a heavy plastic bag on a cutting board. Use a large steel knife or other cooking utility and hit the pecans in an up-and-down motion and crosswise with the blunt side of the knife. It's a quick and easy old-school method to chop up small quantities of nuts.

18. To help eliminate scrubbing of baking pots and casserole dishes grease them with shortening or butter. After cooking your favorite casserole, the baking dish will clean up easily. Just soak in water for a few minutes and wash as usual.

19. When whipping cream, have the bowl, beaters and cream cold before whipping. Cream will whip faster and better. If you over beat the cream, the cream will turn to butter.

20. Buy your favorite cheese in bulk (block) quantity. Grate the entire block and store in sealed, airtight freezer bags and freeze until ready to use. Remove the amount needed and allow it to thaw at room temperature just prior to use.

21. For a thickening agent, use cornstarch and water for clear mixtures. Or use flour and milk for a white and creamy mixture. Or browned flour, water and animal fat for brown gravy.

22. When frying chicken, cooking the chicken on too low a temperature will leave chicken soggy and greasy. With temperature too high, the chicken will cook too fast and the crust will burn before it is done in the middle. I fry my bird on medium high heat!

23. Cool the broth of various cooked meats in the refrigerator to remove the animal fat from the broth. The fat will solidify and rise to the top of the broth when it gets cold to allow for easy removal. I use this technique for all of my soups, gravies, roast, baked chicken, etc.

24. Today, when testing cakes for doneness, I insert a toothpick into the center of the cake. In the olden days, people inserted straw from a broom. Since I've used the same technique, does this make me old? Not!

25. When baking pies, preheat oven – place pricked crust or pie shell into a skillet or on a cookie sheet before pouring mixture in. This guarantees a flaky, crispy, crunchy brown bottom piecrust.

26. Raw eggs in preparing foods—always crack each egg separately and place into a saucer before incorporating into the recipe. This allows you to inspect the egg for freshness and quality. Never use a discolored egg. Example—when I was young, I found an embryo in an egg. It takes awhile to forget the sight of this, believe you me!

27. In cooking, I always measure out all ingredients into separate containers. This method eliminates mistakes and ensures all the ingredients are used.

K's
KITCHEN
SECRETS

CAROLYN MURDOCK MOORE

Table of Contents

My parents...

These are my parents before they married. They courted in the horse-and-buggy days. I bet those were fun times.

Fannie Meek Herring
Born 7-19-1905
Died 9-18-1982

18 Years Old

James Howard Murdock
Born 11-4-1897
Died 10-29-1985

20 Years Old

Carolyn Murdock Has 44 Points For Springfield

SPRINGFIELD, Jan. 5, 1957—Carolyn Murdock, enjoying the finest night of her basketball career, poured in 44 points here tonight as Springfield's girls defeated Allendale-Fairfax, 73-36.

Supporting Miss Murdock was Marguerite Williams, who collected 17 points. Williamson topped the losers with 23.

In the boys' follow-up, Allendale-Fairfax came through with a 62-50 decision as Darrel Williamson shot 18 points and Hare added 16. Scoring honors went to Francis Counts of Springfield with 20 points. Jim Brown got 17 more.

About the night I scored 44 points... <u>The State</u> newspaper honored me the following day in their Sports Highlights. I was both thrilled and honored. Many of these points were free throws from the fouls our opponents inflicted on me. I shot my free throws "Granny-style". Teamwork was the name of the game in order to win. Our guards played good defense and worked the ball to the forwards who tried to score. The forwards on our team were very efficient at working the ball to me under the basket. My junior and senior year basketball first string players included:

Forwards: Marguerite Williams Andrews, Mary Gail Tyler Salley, Willie Evelyn Dyches Hawks, Sue Caughman and Carolyn Murdock Moore.

Guards: Billie Ann Wannamaker, Nancy Counts Stroman, Marie O'Ferrell Knight, Henrietta Gleaton Bundrick. We were coached by Earle "Red" Bethea.

Banana Peanut Butter Snack ℋ

1 large banana
1 heaping tablespoon creamy peanut butter

In a flat surface container mash banana and peanut butter together. Yields 1 cup mixture.

I use this for a breakfast sandwich or on unsalted crackers with a glass of milk. It's filling and nutritional. Works especially well on whole wheat bread and graham crackers.

Cheese Straws

1 stick butter
½ pound grated sharp cheese
1 ½ cups plain flour
½ teaspoon salt
1 teaspoon cayenne pepper (more or less)

Mix all together well. Put in a press or make into rolls and roll ½-inch thick. Slice or use a cake decorating bag to make desired shapes and sizes. Bake at 350° F approximately 15 minutes or until straws are a golden brown. Can double recipe! Yields 1 large platter.

Cocktail Sauce ℋ

¾ cup ketchup
1 tablespoon lemon juice or vinegar
1 tablespoon prepared horseradish
1 teaspoon Worcestershire sauce
4 drops red hot sauce (season to taste)

Mix all ingredients together well and chill until ready to serve. Can double or triple this recipe. Sauce keeps well for one week in the refrigerator.

Delicious Grilled Cheese Sandwich *K*

1 stick melted butter
12 slices bread
6 slices American cheese (not processed cheese food!)
10-inch iron skillet, medium hot

Lightly brush butter over one side of each slice of bread. Place 1 slice of cheese between two slices of bread. Leave butter sides out for grilling. Place 2 sandwiches into skillet, brown well and turn over to brown other side. Do not mash down on the bread while grilling. Remove and repeat process until all 6 sandwiches are browned.

I wish I knew how many of these I've made. Everyone's favorite!

Deviled Egg Dip (Party Style)

8 eggs, boiled and grated
2 cups mayonnaise
2 cups buttermilk
2 packs ranch dressing mix for salads
2 16-ounce cartons sour cream
3 tablespoons chives or onion tops, diced
Lemon pepper to taste
Salt to taste

Mix all ingredients together until smooth. Sprinkle with paprika and diced onion tops or chives. Use chips of your choice. Keep refrigerated until ready to serve. Yields for party of 30.

Party Shrimp Dip ᴷ

Your favorite corn chips
8 ounces cream cheese
1 small can shrimp (about 6 ounces)
½ cup mayonnaise
1 tablespoon onion, grated
1 tablespoon Worcestershire sauce
1 tablespoon lemon juice
2 tablespoons ketchup
½ teaspoon red hot sauce

Combine all but chips together and blend in a blender until smooth. Chill for several hours before serving. Better the second day—so plan ahead!

Ham Cheese Balls (Party Style) ᴷ

½ cup cooked cured ham, grated
1 tablespoon lemon juice
1 teaspoon horseradish
¼ teaspoon liquid smoke
1 teaspoon red hot sauce
8 ounces cream cheese, room temperature
2 teaspoons finely grated onion
1/8 teaspoon salt
1 cup toasted pecans, chopped

Combine all ingredients together except pecans and refrigerate until chilled throughout.

Put pecans into a blender and chop fine. Pour out onto wax paper.

Remove mixture from refrigerator and roll into a ball. Spread out pecans and roll ball into pecans until ball is completely covered in pecans. I press the pecans into the ball.

You can use other cooked meats as a substitution and add other spices. Or double the recipe for large parties.

Ming Cheese

6 ounces cream cheese
2 pounds processed cheese
2 teaspoons garlic powder
1 teaspoon cayenne pepper
2 cups pecans, finely chopped
2 teaspoons paprika
1 teaspoon chili powder

In a large saucepan, combine both cheeses. Put on low heat and stir until melted. Add garlic powder, pepper and pecans. Cool for 20 minutes. Mix chili powder and paprika. Sprinkle onto wax paper. Turn cheese mixture onto wax paper. Make a ball or oblong roll and roll in mixture. Chill thoroughly. Slice as needed. Keep remainder in refrigerator wrapped in wax paper tightly. Keeps well.

Serve with any type of crackers or plain. I have cut mine into cubes holding each with a toothpick.

Party Spiced Pecans

1 egg white
2 tablespoons water
½ cup sugar
¼ teaspoon cinnamon
¼ teaspoon ground cloves
¼ teaspoon allspice
¼ teaspoon salt
2 cups pecan halves

Beat egg white slightly and add water. Combine sugar, cinnamon, cloves, allspice and salt. Add to egg white mixture. Mix well. Let stand until sugar is dissolved, approximately 15 minutes. Dip nuts into mixture. Spread onto an oiled cookie sheet. Place flat side of nut down. Bake at 250°F until golden (about 1 hour). Cool! Store in an airtight container. Yields 2 cups. Double or triple recipe for large parties.

Sugar Coated Peanuts

1 cup water
1 teaspoon vanilla flavoring
2 cups sugar
4 cups raw peanuts

Combine ingredients and mix together. In an iron skillet, cook slowly until water is gone and getting hard. Stir often. Pour mixture onto a greased pan and bake for 30 to 40 minutes at 350° F. Cool completely before storing in jars. Keep in a dry place and enjoy!

This recipe makes great gifts for Christmas. Place into decorative containers. Will keep for a long time.

Tuna Salad for Four ᴷ

1 can tuna, packed in water, drained
1 can tuna, packed in oil, drained
4 eggs, boiled and chopped
2 tablespoons sweet pickle relish
1 teaspoon mustard
Salt and pepper to taste
1 apple, chopped (optional)
1 tablespoon dill pickle juice
1 teaspoon of your favorite meat spice
¼ cup chopped nuts, optional
¼ cup mayonnaise, more or less

Using a fork, combine tuna in medium mixing bowl; add rest of ingredients. Add about ¼ cup mayonnaise according to taste and mix until blended well.

Notes:

Horse-N-Buggy Days...

My dad, James Howard Murdock.
Looks like fun. I can imagine my mother sitting
next to him on their way to a special event.

Grandfather Murdock's 1927 Touring Car and family members.
Shown are my dad's sister Mabel Murdock Moody
and her two children Frances and Ruth.

My dad, James Howard Murdock and his first shotgun.

My dad, James Howard Murdock and his sheep.

Basic Thick Vanilla Milk Shake ᵏ

1 pint vanilla ice cream
¾ cup milk
2 teaspoons vanilla flavoring

Mix all ingredients in blender and blend until smooth.

Make your own flavors. For chocolate, add 3 tablespoons of Chocolate Syrup ᵏ. For pineapple, add ½ cup crushed pineapple plus ¾ cup pineapple juice, omitting the milk. Use your favorite flavor of ice cream and follow recipe. For a thick rich malted milk shake, add 1 tablespoon of malt before blending.

Hot Chocolate ᵏ

4 cups milk
4 tablespoons Chocolate Syrup ᵏ
4 tablespoons whipped cream or whipped topping

In a one-quart saucepan combine milk and syrup. Heat until just under boiling point. Remove from stove. Pour into 4 cups. Place whipped cream on top. Yields 4 servings.

Punch

2 46-ounce cans pineapple juice
2 46-ounce cans fruit punch
2 16-ounce bottles ginger ale
2 12-ounce cans frozen orange juice

Mix all together but ginger ale and chill! When ready to serve mix with chilled ginger ale. Makes about 2 gallons of punch.

Large Party Punch

8 large cans frozen orange juice, diluted according to directions on can
8 large cans frozen lemon juice, diluted according to directions on can
8 quarts pineapple juice
2 gallons water
Add sugar to taste
8 quarts ginger ale
6 quarts of frozen orange sherbet
10 one-gallon containers

Mix fruit juice, water and ginger ale. Add sugar to taste. Refrigerate punch until serving time in the gallon containers. Just before serving, add orange sherbet to center of punch bowl. Yields 10 gallons.

Lime Wedding Punch $\mathcal{K}$

½ gallon lime sherbet
2 quarts ginger ale

Put ½ gallon lime sherbet in a large punch bowl. Pour ginger ale over the sherbet—the ale will melt the sherbet. Serve punch a little lumpy. May want to soften the sherbet for 15 minutes prior to making the punch. Dunk sherbet a few times into the ale to mix the punch.

This was used for my sister's wedding. I've used this many times. Serve for all occasions. Spike with a cup of gin or vodka if desired. Can also make a float by adding 2 scoops sherbet to a cup of ginger ale.

Ronald's Southern Sweetened Iced Tea

2 family-sized tea bags
1 quart water
1 cup sugar

Place water into a 1 ½-quart saucepan and bring to a rolling boil. Add tea bags, cover and simmer for 10 minutes. Remove from heat. When cooled, remove tea bags and add sugar, mixing well. Pour mixture into a one-gallon container. Fill container with water. Yields 1 gallon.

Spiced Tea Mix

1 cup instant lemon tea
½ teaspoon cinnamon
¼ teaspoon cloves
1 package unsweetened orange drink mix

Combine all ingredients into blender and blend well. Store in a dry container. When ready to use: Mix 1 teaspoon of mix per 6 to 8-ounce glass of water. Serve hot or cold. Yields 6 quarts.

Charles' Brewed Tea

5 individual tea bags
Water
¾ cup sugar

Place tea bags into electric drip coffee maker. Add 4 to 5 cups of water to coffee maker and brew (just like making coffee). When tea has finished brewing, add tea and sugar to ½ gallon container. Fill with water to make ½ gallon. Tea is always best the next day after it is brewed!

Making Frozen Drinks (general)

Measure out all ingredients for a particular drink and pour into 8-ounce glass filled with ice. Place all contents into blender and blend on high for 10 to 15 seconds to achieve desired consistency. Will have to "jog" blender to thoroughly blend all of the small ice chunks. Pour into serving glasses.

This works well for daiquiris, margaritas, hurricanes, and piña coladas. I prefer frozen virgin drinks, so you can figure out my favorites.

Bloody Mary (or Maria)

Highball or Collins glass (12 ounce)
1 ounce vodka (or tequila for a Maria)
2 dashes black pepper
2 dashes salt
2 dashes celery salt
4 drops Worcestershire sauce
1 drop hot sauce (or more if you like it hot!)
Tomato juice

In an ice-filled glass, mix all ingredients. Add tomato juice to fill glass. Stir and garnish with celery stick and lime. This is a very tasty drink without the vodka or tequila.

Fuzzy Navel

Highball glass
1 ounce vodka
1 ounce peach Schnapps
Orange juice

Using a highball glass with ice, add 1 ounce each peach schnapps and vodka and fill remainder with orange juice.

Hot Toddy For The Body

1 ounce bourbon
1 teaspoon honey

Add ingredients to hot coffee mug and add hot water to fill.

Hurricane

1 ounce light rum
1 ounce dark rum
2 ounces sweet and sour
2 ounces orange juice
2 ounces pineapple juice
½ ounce Grenadine

Shake and strain. Top with a splash of 151 proof rum. Garnish with cherry, orange or pineapple. This is a very tasty drink without the rum.

*H. Ronald and Danna Davenport Moore
Their day, July 20, 1991*

Kamikaze

1 ounce vodka
½ ounce Triple Sec
½ ounce lime juice
Splash of sweet and sour

Shake and strain.

Lime Daiquiri

1 ounce light rum
½ ounce lime juice
1 ½ ounces sweet and sour
1 teaspoon sugar or corn syrup
Lime wedge for garnish

Add ice and blend to serve frozen or mix and pour to serve on the rocks. Garnish with a lime wedge. This is a very tasty drink without the rum.

Long Island Tea

½ ounce vodka
½ ounce gin
½ ounce rum
½ ounce Triple Sec
2 ounces sweet and sour
Splash of coke
Lemon for garnish

Shake and strain. Serve on the rocks. Garnish with lemon wheel.

Margarita

Prepare serving glass with salted rim.
(Dip in water or lemon juice first so the salt will stick.)
1 ounce tequila
½ ounce Triple Sec
1 ½ ounces sweet and sour
½ ounce lime juice
Lime wedge for garnish

Shake well while straining into glass. Serve on the rocks and garnish with a lime wedge.

Frozen Piña Coladas ᴷ

4 ounces cream of coconut
8 ounces pineapple juice
6 ounces rum, gin or vodka
3 cups ice

In a blender on high speed, mix all ingredients for 30 seconds. Serve in a tall glass. Decorate with pineapple chunks and a cherry. Yields 4 servings.

Virgin Piña Colada Shake ᴷ

3 ounces cream of coconut
½ cup pineapple juice
2 cups cold milk
6 scoops vanilla ice cream

In a blender, blend for 30 seconds or until frothy. Yields 4 servings.

Piña Colada

1 ounce rum
2 ounces cream of coconut
3 ounces pineapple juice
Pineapple wedge and cherry to garnish

Blend rum, coconut, and pineapple juice. Pour into a glass. Garnish with a pineapple wedge/cherry. Can add 4 or 5 fresh strawberries just prior to blending. This is a very good drink without the rum.

Screwdriver

Highball glass
1 ounce vodka
Fill with orange juice

Shake and strain. Serve on the rocks.

Sex On The Beach

½ ounce vodka
½ ounce Midori
½ ounce raspberry Schnapps
½ ounce pineapple juice

Shake and strain. Serve on the rocks.

Snakebite

1 ounce tequila
1 ounce peppermint Schnapps

Shake and strain.

Tequila Sunrise

Collins glass
1 ounce tequila
½ ounce Grenadine
Fill with orange juice
Cherry

Fill glass with ice. Add ingredients. Stir and garnish with a cherry.

Vodka Collins

1 ounce vodka
2 ounces sweet and sour

Shake well while straining into glass. Fill with lemon-lime carbonated beverage. Garnish with a cherry.

White Russian

Highball glass
1 ounce vodka
½ ounce Kahlua
½ ounce cream or milk

Blend, or shake and serve on the rocks.

Notes:

Hugh McMillan Murdock
1948

In memory of my brothers...

James Clinton Murdock and
Hugh McMillan Murdock

James Clinton Murdock. Born October 4, 1925. Died October 4, 1925. Buried in City Cemetery, Kosciusko, Mississippi.

James Clinton Murdock, my oldest brother, was born and died the same day. My mother never got over or fully recovered from losing her first child. I have a document that my mother wrote entitled "Memories Linger". In it she tells about only getting to hold James Clinton once. This document was dated many years after his death. She said that he was a beautiful baby. He was a blue baby. Back then, current medical technology could not correct this condition.

Hugh McMillan Murdock. Born July 27, 1930. Died January 5, 1998. Buried in Parkway Cemetery, Kosciusko, Mississippi.

Hugh McMillan Murdock, my brother, was a devoted son, brother and uncle. My mother said he prayed every day for a baby brother. Later, after my mother had just given birth to me, my brother came to her bedside with a red rose in his hand to give to his new baby brother he thought. He asked my mother if this was his new baby brother. She said, "No, this is your new baby sister." Mother said Hugh had tears rolling down his cheeks. Then, as he flicked the tears away he said, "Well, that's alright—she'll be sweet." From that day on there was a special bond between us until the day he died. We did have our differences of opinion though.

Hugh was a very generous person with his time, love and money. He would sacrifice, giving up one thing for the sake of another. As a child at Christmas and only having a quarter to spend he would stretch it and buy five gifts. That's one gift for each member in our family. It wasn't the amount of the gift but the thought that counted. Mother always taught us that Christmas was not our birthday, but the birthday of Jesus, our Lord and Savior.

Hugh was most protective of me. He always had my best interest at heart. Upon high school graduation, he enlisted in the Navy for four years of active duty. He was always bringing the family beautiful souvenirs from the fourteen countries he toured. Souvenirs such as foreign dolls, wooden shoes, perfumes, jewelry, coverlets, bedspreads, silver cigarette cases, silk scarves, tapestries, a dragon ware demitasse tea set and hand-carved wooden shoes. Most of these items I still have today.

Upon departure of the Navy, he joined our family in Springfield, South Carolina. He had become an excellent dancer while in the service, having been taught by a professional. He asked me one day if I would like to learn all of the dances that he knew and be the best on the dance floor? My reply of course was, "Yes!" He taught me the sophisticated style of the Carolina Shag with twenty different moves, the Rumba, the Waltz, the Bunny Hop, the Polka, the Shuffle, the Two Step (a slow dance with the hold step and walk step) and the Charleston. Later, I added the Twist, the Half Twist and the Cha-Cha. Hugh was thoughtful, and took me dancing from time to time. People couldn't believe that a brother would take the time to dance with his sister. His reply was always "I taught her, she's one of the best." Hugh and I made a video of dancing together on December 25, 1995 of which I cherish and watch often.

Hugh spent most of his later life in New Orleans in the vicinity of the French Quarters (Esplanade and Royal Street). He retired from Martin Marietta's Space Division as an Expeditor. He enjoyed doing good deeds for others, especially in times of crisis. He loved to garden both flowers and vegetables, travel, and play card games. He loved the art of dancing, attending concerts, civic affairs and collecting antiques. My sons called him Uncle Brother. Hugh loved my two sons as if they were his own. Always showering them with material things. He spent nearly every holiday in or around my home and with our parents. He often brought friends to Kosciusko to enjoy my cooking, baking and canned goods. Of course, I would always cook his favorites. He took off a week each time I had a baby to be "the proud uncle." He wanted a namesake so I named my second son after him. I took Hugh unconditionally. His strengths far outweighed his weaknesses. He will always have a special place in my heart.

Beef and Vegetable Soup K

6 quarts cooked beef roast, cubed (4 medium roast)
8 quarts tomatoes
2 quarts string beans
8 pounds Irish potatoes, quartered
5 pounds onions, sliced and cut crosswise once
3 pounds carrots, sliced ¼ inch thick
8 cans whole corn
4 cans cream style corn
1 can English peas
10 ounces Worcestershire
6 ounces hot sauce
2 tablespoons sugar, more or less depending on taste
Salt and pepper to taste
1 quart celery, chopped
4 quarts beef roast broth (saved from cooking roast)

Combine all together and put into two sixteen-quart containers, except cubed roast. Simmer for 1 hour and then add roast. Simmer for an additional 30 minutes. Yields 28 quarts for freezer.

Cool roast broth and skim off fat from top (always comes to the surface when chilled). Saves on calories as well as your health. Serve with corn bread or crackers. I've been making this for my freezer for thirty years. Really is nice to wonder what I will have for lunch then bring out a quart of this tasty soup to heat and serve.

Cabbage Slaw ℋ

1 medium head of cabbage, grated on hand grater on course side
3 carrots, grated on fine side of hand grater
½ cup sweet relish
3 tablespoons sugar, sprinkled over cabbage
1 cup mayonnaise (more or less)
2 tablespoons dill pickle juice
Salt and pepper to taste

Mix all together well and chill. Keep refrigerated. Will last for several days. Serves 12-14.

Pappy Murdock's Beef & Vegetable Stew

1 5-pound roast, cooked & shredded (save broth, cool and skim off fat)
3 large 16-ounce cans tomatoes
4 16-ounce cans cream style corn
2 medium onions, chopped
Salt and pepper to taste
1 quart beef broth
¼ cup sugar

Combine all ingredients and simmer for 45 minutes. Should be thick.

This is better the second day after cooking than the first day. My dad would make this in large quantities and can in big mouth jars. He also would add carrots to the stew, especially when the price of roast got more costly and required stretching the budget. Yields 12 servings.

Chicken Salad 𝒦

4 cups cooked, diced, cold chicken
½ cup sweet pickle relish
½ cup diced celery
3 tablespoons minced dill pickles
1 cup apples, chopped, optional
1 cup mayonnaise, more or less
1 cup walnuts, chopped
¾ teaspoon salt
½ teaspoon black pepper
1 teaspoon prepared mustard
3 tablespoons lemon juice

In a three-quart mixing bowl, mix all ingredients together and mix well. Add additional lemon juice to taste. Chill until ready to serve. Yields 7 ½ cups.

Congealed Strawberry Salad 𝒦

Prepare 4 hours before serving.
2 3-ounce packages strawberry gelatin
2 cups boiling water
2 ¼ cups ice cold water
3 bananas, sliced 1/8-inch thick
2 cups halved seeded grapes
Whipped cream or topping

In a two-quart mixing bowl combine boiling water and gelatin. Stir constantly until dissolved. Add cold water and mix well. Pour mixture into a two-quart casserole dish. Place into refrigerator. When this mixture barely begins to set up (congeal), stir in bananas and grapes. Refrigerate until mixture is firm. Top each serving with whipped cream. Yield 8 servings.

Can use any flavor of gelatin with chopped nuts, fruit cocktail, drained, other combinations of fruits. Your choice.

English Pea Salad ℋ

15-ounce can English peas, chilled
3 boiled eggs, chopped and chilled
1 tablespoon onion, chopped
1/3 cup celery, diced and chilled
2 tablespoons pimento pepper, chopped
1 tablespoon dill pickle juice
1/3 cup mayonnaise
Salt and pepper to taste

Mix all together well. Keep chilled until serving time. Serves 6.

Fruit Mold Salad ℋ

3-ounce package orange gelatin
2 tablespoons sugar
1 ¼ cups boiling water
1/2 cups cold water
2 oranges, peeled and sectioned
1 ¼ cups seedless grapes, halved
2/3 cup flaked coconut
1 cup whipping cream, whipped
1 cup pineapple slices, chopped and drained

Dissolve gelatin and sugar in boiling water. Stir in cold water and chill until the consistency of egg whites. Stir in oranges, grapes, pineapple and coconut. Fold in whipped cream gently. Pour or spoon into an oiled mold and chill. Yields 8 servings.

Healthy Carrot Salad *K*

1 pound carrots, washed & finely grated
2/3 cup white or brown raisins, soaked in cold water 5 minutes
2/3 cup crushed pineapple, drained
½ cup celery, finely chopped
1 teaspoon fresh lemon juice (optional)
Mayonnaise
Red cherries for garnish

In a large bowl, combine all together. Add just enough mayonnaise to hold together. Serve in a pretty bowl or as individual servings. Garnish with a cherry or cherry halves.

My mother always told us that carrots were good for our eyesight and raisins are a good source of iron as well. Mothers won't tell you wrong.

Pear and Cheese Salad *K*

6 lettuce leaves, cupped on a salad plate
12 pear halves
1 cup grated cheese
Mayonnaise
6 maraschino cherries, whole

Place 2 pear halves on lettuce leaves and sprinkle cheese over the top of each. Add about ½ a teaspoon of mayonnaise in the center. Top with a cherry. Serve chilled. Yields 6 servings.

Macaroni Salad ᴷ

2 cups cooked macaroni, chilled

Note: Boil macaroni, dash of salt, water with 1 teaspoon oil to prevent macaroni from sticking together (approximately 10 minutes).

3 boiled eggs (boil for 10 minutes), diced
1 medium onion, diced
¼ cup sweet relish, chopped
¼ cup dill pickle, chopped
1 teaspoon mustard
Salt and pepper to taste
¼ cup bell pepper, diced
1 tablespoon lemon juice (to enhance flavor)
4 tablespoons pimento pepper
Mayonnaise

Combine all ingredients in a large salad bowl. Toss with ½ cup mayonnaise. Keep cold until ready to serve. Makes 6 servings.

For variations, add two cups cooked cubed chicken and two tablespoons fresh lemon juice.

Pineapple Salad ᴷ

6 lettuce leaves, cupped on a salad plate
6 slices pineapple
1 cup grated cheese
Mayonnaise
6 maraschino cherries, whole

Place 2 pineapple slices on lettuce leaves and sprinkle cheese over the top of each. Add ½ teaspoon of mayonnaise in the center. Top with a cherry. Serve chilled. Yields 6 servings.

Ritzy Lime Salad ᴷ

3 ½-ounce package lime gelatin
8 ounces cottage cheese
½ cup chopped pecans or walnuts
½ cup sliced maraschino cherries
½ cup pineapple, cubed, tidbits, or crushed
5 drops green food coloring
8-ounce container whipped topping

Mix lime gelatin and cottage cheese together in large bowl. Add remaining ingredients except whipped topping and food coloring. Add two mixtures together and fold together. Add food coloring and fold. Add whipped topping and fold in over and over until smooth. Garnish with chipped cherries. Makes 8 servings.

Quick and easy but elegant...fit for a king! Double recipe for large crowd! When I'm planning my special occasion menus my sons, Charles and Hugh Ronald always remind me "Don't forget the lime salad Mama!" It's splendid for any occasion!

Plain Fruit Salad ᴷ

1 cup red delicious apples, chopped but not too small
½ cup orange slices, cut in half
½ cup fresh pineapple chunks
8 maraschino cherries, cut in half
¼ cup walnuts or pecans
½ cup grapes, seeded and chopped in half
3 tablespoons of sugar (or sugar substitute)

Mix all ingredients together and sprinkle sugar over top and toss. Serve plain or add enough mayonnaise to mix. Keep refrigerated.

Potato Salad ℋ

4 Irish potatoes, peeled and quartered
4 boiled eggs, peeled, diced and cooled
1 medium onion, diced
½ cup sweet relish
1 teaspoon yellow prepared mustard
Salt and pepper to taste
¼ cup bell pepper (optional)
¼ cup dill pickle, diced
Mayonnaise
1 tablespoon red pimento pepper, chopped (for garnish)

Boil potatoes until barely tender, drain water and cool. Add remaining ingredients, except pimento, with mayonnaise and mix together well. Add enough mayonnaise to hold mixture together. Garnish with red pimento pepper and swirl once.

I always have all ingredients cold to avoid spoilage. It is better to add more mayonnaise later than to try to remove mayonnaise from this mixture! Be careful on how much you add the first time. May garnish with paprika.

Shrimp Garden Salad ℋ

4 cups lettuce, any or all kinds mixed together
1 small onion, sliced thin
1 cup celery, diced
6 red radishes, sliced
2 medium tomatoes, cut in wedges
1 pound medium shrimp (cooked in shrimp boil, peeled and chilled)
Juice of one lemon
½ cup Italian or Thousand Island salad dressing

In a large mixing bowl, combine all ingredients with ½ cup Italian or Thousand Island salad dressing. Mix together. Chill before serving.

Supreme Fruit Salad 𝒦

1 pint of whipping cream
¼ cup sugar
1 teaspoon vanilla flavoring
3 cups red delicious apples, chopped but not too small
2 cups oranges, peeled & cross cut with scissors
2 cups pineapple, fresh cut into chunks
1 cup maraschino cherries, cut in half
1 ½ cups chopped walnuts or pecans
1 ½ cups grapes, white or dark, seeded
¼ cup sugar (sprinkle over fruit)

Whip whipping cream while slowly adding ¼ cup sugar and 1 teaspoon vanilla flavoring. Don't whip so long until the cream stiffens and makes butter!

With spatula, turn out whipping cream over fruit mixtures and fold. Refrigerate until serving time. Yields 20 servings.

This is a favorite at my home on Thanksgiving, Christmas and Easter. It's an all occasion salad. Can cut in half if too much for your family.

Oil & Vinegar Salad Dressing 𝒦

½ cup vegetable oil
1 cup vinegar
½ cup sugar
1 clove garlic, crushed
Salt and pepper to taste
Juice of 1 lemon

Mix all together and put into a container. Shake the container before using.

Honey Mustard Dressing ℋ

2 cups olive oil
½ cup apple cider vinegar
2 ¼ cups honey
½ cup fancy mustard
1 ½ cups mayonnaise
¼ teaspoon garlic powder

In a two-quart mixing bowl, mix all ingredients together. Stir until smooth. Keep refrigerated. Yields 1 ½ quarts.

Buttermilk Dressing ℋ

2 cups mayonnaise
2 cups buttermilk
2 tablespoons minced parsley
2 tablespoons minced onion
1 teaspoon apple cider vinegar
2 teaspoons lemon juice
½ teaspoon garlic powder

In a two-quart mixing bowl, combine mayonnaise and buttermilk. Mix until smooth. Add rest of ingredients and mix well. Refrigerate until ready to use. Yields 1 quart.

French Dressing

1 cup virgin olive oil
1 cup sugar
1 cup ketchup
1 teaspoon salt
½ teaspoon black pepper
½ teaspoon prepared mustard
1 teaspoon onion powder
½ teaspoon red hot sauce
1/8 teaspoon garlic powder
1 teaspoon Worcestershire sauce
1 cup hot apple cider vinegar

In a large-mouth quart jar, blend oil and sugar. Add remaining ingredients (except vinegar). Mix well. Add vinegar and stir well. Refrigerate until needed. Yields 2 ¾ cups.

Thousand Island Dressing 𝒦

2 cups mayonnaise
1/8 cup ketchup
¼ cup sweet pickle juice
½ cup sweet pickle relish
2 tablespoons minced dill pickle
2 tablespoons prepared mustard
3 tablespoons dill pickle juice
2 tablespoons lemon juice
1 tablespoon pimento, minced
¼ teaspoon chili powder
1 tablespoon sugar
2-quart mixing bowl

In mixing bowl combine mayonnaise and ketchup and mix until well blended. Add rest of ingredients and mix well. Chill. Keep refrigerated. Yields 1 quart.

Notes:

Notes:

My family...

*My mother & father, my brother Hugh,
myself (smallest), my sister Margaret,
not pictured -- my sister Elsie.*

In memory of my parents...

James Howard Murdock, "Pappy" and Fannie Meek Herring Murdock, "Grandma"

Pappy was born November 4, 1897 in Uniontown, Alabama. He died October 29, 1985 and is buried in Parkway Cemetery in Kosciusko, Mississippi. His parents were Hugh McMillan and Margaret Starr Murdock, descendants of Robert and Elizabeth Murdock, who came to America by way of Ireland. The Murdock family came from respectable ancestry—the covenanters of Scotland. The covenanters were historically known as "conscience men."

Pappy was raised in the Youngstown area of Ohio in his early years. He later moved to Waynesboro, Mississippi, to Ohio again and finally returned to Kosciusko, Mississippi. His mother and father purchased large tracts of land. He shared a farmer's life, raising cattle and shearing sheep for market. Pappy quit school because of his parents' ill health and became caretaker of the family farm. His father, a former schoolteacher, home schooled him. My father said he worked hard on the farm and even considered that he was a successful farmer until the Great Depression. And there were other interferences. He married my mother, Fannie Meek Herring on January 15, 1925. Grandma was born August 19, 1905 in Kosciusko, Mississippi. She died September 18, 1982 and is buried in Parkway Cemetery in Kosciusko, Mississippi. My mother was the daughter of I. A. "Ike" and Minnie Leola Herring, whose estate was approximately ½ mile from the Murdock estate. Properness was the going thing

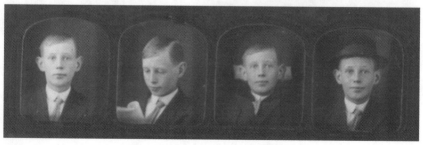

My dad, James Howard Murdock
1906, 9 years old

in their day. I have the letters that my dad sent by messengers to my mother asking her for a date. The messenger waited for a reply.

In the early 1930's, daddy purchased land from his father-in-law across from the present day community of Tracewood and built our family home. I was the only child to be born at the family home in the sentimental spool bed. This beautiful spool bed today resides in my guest bedroom. After leaving his family farm, Pappy began to work at various construction jobs as a union carpenter. He helped build many of the finest homes in the Kosciusko area. My dad helped to build three defense plants located in Oak Ridge TN, Aiken SC, and Camp Shelby MS.

My parents opened and closed each day by reading The Bible with us and praying on our knees. We couldn't get up until mother said "Amen" -- even if the school bus was blowing the horn. We were brought up on faith. Speaking of faith...

Each week, the merchants of Kosciusko carried on a promotion. With every purchase during the week, respective stores would give their customers half a numbered raffle ticket while putting the other half into a box for the big drawing. On Wednesday night, the tickets from all the stores were recombined at the Pix movie theater. The prize to be coveted was a shiny, new bicycle. My brother Hugh really wanted to have a bicycle... My mother encouraged him to have faith and told him that she sincerely believed that he would be a winner. On the night of the drawing, Mother and the rest of the family at home got down on our knees and had prayer, thanking the Lord for all of His blessings, and finally petitioning that my brother would have the winning ticket. Everyone dressed for Wednesday night prayer meeting and went to church. My brother thought that he would be dropped off at the theater so he could wait for the drawing. He was a little surprised to find out that he was going to an hour of prayer meeting first. Mother told him that he could leave when the last hymn was in progress and he didn't know an hour could last so long! Finally the last hymn came and he bolted three and one-half blocks to the theater to be there for the 8:00 P.M. drawing. I didn't see how he would make it in time... We left church and went to the theater to pick up my brother. As we rounded the corner, there he was proudly displaying his new bicycle in the street. We were ecstatic. On the way home, we learned that my brother had so much faith about winning the bicycle that he even brought a rope to secure the bike to the car. When we arrived home that night, my brother wanted to ride his bike immediately. But Mother said firmly that we must first thank the Lord for making this possible. The funny thing about this story is that we weren't allowed to go to the movies!

My mother told us every day she loved us. She was a very giving person. She wanted all the little children to hear about Jesus. She helped support the Buffalo Church near our home by collecting songbooks, religious material and anything else that she felt the people could benefit from. When she learned that a church a few miles from home didn't have a piano, Grandma gave the church our piano purchased years earlier for my sister. We were always invited to the church revivals at Buffalo. My sister was invited to sing solos.

I don't recall ever hearing my dad say that he loved me. He didn't have to since he showed his love to us in many ways. I learned many things from my Dad. During our frequent trips to the swamp (a.k.a. Munson's), he taught me the correct way to shoot a gun. He taught me to float in the crystal clear water at the canal—telling me that I would never drown if I could float. On one of our outings in the swamp, we found ourselves surrounded by high waters. Daddy taught me to cross the river on a log using canes to balance the log. Although I was scared to death, we safely made it to the other side. Sometimes we would walk the railroad tracks to visit my aunt. He would tell me to be on the lookout for money—that I just might find some today. Then I carefully scanned the railroad tracks for money. Later I always found some change. One day I caught my dad flipping the money down the tracks and the game was over.

My mother was a teacher in the beginner's class for twenty-three years at the First Presbyterian Church in Kosciusko. My dad taught the young men's class for a period of time. We had family sword drills of The Bible, spelling bees, and played hide and seek, baseball, and all kinds of card games. Rook was the family favorite. Mother and Daddy were great cooks, bringing down the family favorites from other generations, which I'm honored to share with you. We made homemade ice cream very often. Taffy pulling, peanut brittle, chocolate fudge, hot chocolate with whipped cream and fellowship was the name of the game in the Murdock home. We had large family gatherings, and just never knew how many to cook for. Somehow everyone had plenty to eat. I did my share of chores in and around the house from a young age. Mother gave me great support with things I wanted to achieve in life. After marrying and having our two sons, mother wanted Charles to come and live with her. I told her I wanted to raise my children, but I would share my sons with she and my dad on weekends and holidays. This I did all of their lives. Mother and daddy taught us all of the good values in life. High on their etiquette list were good manners at the table and in public. And to treat other people as you would like to be treated. My mother said that this reciprocity would not always happen in return, but to pray that the Lord would change their ways. Teaching your children from birth until they are eighteen years of age are the parents duties in order for the children to be able to maintain in the outside society called "the real world." My mother believed "a parents life is a child's guidebook."

My dad started teaching me to drive at age five by allowing me to guide the car. By age seven, I was guiding and using the foot feed. By age ten, I drove for myself the very first time. He told a friend of his that if I passed his test, then I could pass anyone's test. Needless to say, I got my license at fourteen in the state of South Carolina.

When I lost my parents, I lost the best friends that I will ever have in life.

Hush Yo' Mouth Puppies 𝒦

My sons say they've eaten many, but these are the best!

1 ½ cups self-rising meal
1 teaspoon baking powder, heaping
¾ cup self-rising flour
1 teaspoon sugar
½ teaspoon black pepper
½ teaspoon garlic powder (optional)
½ teaspoon salt
2 eggs, beaten
2 large finely grated onions (juicy pulp)
3 tablespoons hot fish oil

Mix together dry ingredients. Make a cup-shaped hole in the dry ingredients and add eggs and onions. Mix well with fork or spoon. Add oil to mixture and mix well.

Spoon the hushpuppies one at a time into medium to hot oil using a teaspoon-sized amount. Remove from grease and drain when hushpuppies are medium brown.

If batter is too thick to mix, add small amount of buttermilk. If batter is not thick enough, add a little more corn meal. The amount serves about 10 people.

Garlic Butter Spread 𝒦

1 stick butter, room temperature
1 ½ teaspoons garlic powder

In a pint-sized mixing bowl, combine butter and garlic powder. Mix well. Yields ½ cup.

I place this spread liberally between sliced loaves of French bread. Keeping bread intact, wrap and seal bread in foil. Heat at 350° F for 20 minutes. Serve immediately.

Southern Corn Sticks 𝒦

½ cup self-rising flour
½ cup self-rising corn meal
1 teaspoon sugar
2 teaspoons baking powder
1/8 teaspoon salt
½ cup buttermilk
1 egg, beaten
2 tablespoons vegetable oil
2 6-section cast iron corn stick bakers, well greased and hot

Preheat oven to 400° F

Combine dry ingredients and mix well. Add egg, buttermilk and oil. Beat with a spoon until smooth. Fill hot greased sections 2/3 full and bake for 10 minutes until brown! Yields 12 corn sticks.

Every time I made these while my sons where young I'd end up with two or three on the bread plate when dinner was to be served. Of course, they would have an innocent look on their faces. Would probably be the same way today if they were around when these are baked.

Cracklin' Bread 𝒦

Yields one 10-inch skillet

1 ½ cups self-rising corn meal
1 tablespoon self-rising flour, heaping
1 teaspoon baking powder
Dash of salt
1 ¼ cups buttermilk
1 egg
1 ½ cups cracklings
¼ cup oil

Preheat oven to 350° F

Combine corn meal, flour, baking powder and salt in a medium mixing bowl and mix well. Add buttermilk and beat for 2 minutes. Add egg and whip until mixture is uniform. Add cracklings and stir.

Have skillet hot and add oil to skillet! When oil is hot, pour ½ of oil in corn meal mixture and mix well. Wipe skillet with a wet cloth. Put a pinch of corn meal in hot skillet oil and brown the meal! Pour corn bread batter into skillet and place into 350° F oven. Cook for 20 minutes. Remove and brown. Turn out on a 10-inch plate and serve while warm. Yields 8 servings.

¼ cup oil is the amount you want for the recipe. Oil expands when heated. It's important to put oil into skillet and heat to get correct amount. Adding the hot oil to the mixture helps the bread turn out crunchy around the edges.

Buttermilk 𝒦

1 cup milk
1 teaspoon lemon juice or 1 teaspoon vinegar

Stir ingredients together well. Finished product—your own buttermilk for cooking!

Skillet Corn Bread K

Yields one 10-inch skillet

1 ½ cups self-rising corn meal
1 tablespoon self-rising flour, heaping
1 teaspoon baking powder
Dash of salt
1 ¼ cups buttermilk
1 egg
¼ cup oil

Preheat oven to 350° F

Combine corn meal, flour, baking powder and salt in a medium mixing bowl and mix well. Add buttermilk and beat for 2 minutes. Add egg and whip until mixture is uniform.

Have skillet hot and add oil to skillet! When oil is hot, pour ½ of oil into corn meal mixture and mix well. Wipe rim of skillet with a wet cloth to remove excess oil. Put a pinch of corn meal into hot skillet oil and brown! Pour corn bread batter into skillet and place into 350° F oven. Bake for 20 minutes. Remove and brown. Turn out on a 10-inch plate and serve while warm. Yields 8 servings.

Use ¼ cup oil for this recipe. Oil expands when heated. It's important to put oil into skillet and heat to get correct amount. Adding the hot oil to the mixture helps the bread turn out tender inside and crunchy around the edges.

Corn Bread *K*

¼ cup vegetable oil
2 cups self-rising corn meal
2 teaspoons self-rising flour
1 teaspoon baking powder
1/8 teaspoon salt
1 1/3 cups buttermilk
1 egg, beaten

Step 1: Have 10-inch iron skillet hot with vegetable oil and preheat oven to 350° F.

Step 2: In a mixing bowl combine corn meal, flour, baking powder and salt. Mix well.

Step 3: Add buttermilk to Step 2 mixture and beat for 1 minute. Add egg and beat for 2 minutes. I beat the mixture with a large spoon.

Step 4: Add ¾ of the hot oil from skillet to mixture, leaving rest of hot oil in skillet. Add a sprinkle of corn meal to the hot oil in the skillet, stir and let the meal brown.

Step 5: Pour mixture into evenly distributed oil and browned corn meal mixture. Place into 350° F pre-heated oven. When mixture begins to form a cracked look on top of bread (does not jiggle), brown well and turn out on a bread plate (bottom side up).

Use a good brand of self–rising corn meal. I do not sift my ingredients. Yields 8 servings.

Sour Cream Muffins

1 cup self-rising corn meal
½ cup sour cream
2 eggs, beaten
½ cup vegetable oil
1 small can cream-style corn

Mix all together, beating well. Pour into small muffin tins ½ full that have been sprayed with non-stick or hot and greased. Bake at 350° F until done. Broil to a golden brown. Remove from pan and turn upright. We do not cook these very often—they are sinful!

Exotic "Skillet" German Corn Bread

1 ½ cups self-rising corn meal
2 eggs, beaten
½ cups vegetable oil
8-ounce can creamed style corn
1 cup French onion dip (or sour cream)
1 large onion, chopped

Mix all together and beat well. Preheat a 10-inch skillet with 3 table-spoons of hot oil and sprinkle 1/8 teaspoon corn meal. Brown corn meal until golden and then pour mixture into skillet. Bake at 400° F for 30 to 35 minutes until brown. Turn onto a flat plate.

I've always had many compliments when I serve this corn bread. My guests usually want the recipe. They have even asked to take the leftovers home with them.

Mama's Biscuits ^K

1/3 cup shortening, room temperature
2 cups flour, self-rising
¼ teaspoon baking powder
¾ cup buttermilk
Butter, melted for brushing

Preheat oven to 350° F

In a mixing bowl, cut shortening into dry mixture with a pastry cutter, or two knives, or fork until mixture looks like small peas. Add buttermilk, mixing until dry ingredients are moistened.

On a floured cloth, turn dough out. Sprinkle flour over dough and knead a few times. Make a ball and pat or roll out with a rolling pin to ¾-inch thickness. Cut with a 2 ½-inch round cutter. Place biscuits onto a well-greased baking pan or into an iron skillet baker. Bake at 350° F for 10 to 12 minutes. Brush melted butter onto biscuits just before browning. Yields 10 to 12 biscuits.

This recipe can also be used for a top crust for fruit cobblers—peach, blackberry, apple, pear, etc. Add butter, vanilla-cinnamon-sugar sprinkle over top of crust.

Garlic Butter ^K

½ cup butter, softened
2 tablespoons fresh chives, chopped
1 teaspoon garlic powder (or 3 cloves minced garlic)
1/8 teaspoon salt

Using a fork, cream butter until fluffy. Add remaining ingredients and blend well. Chill several hours if using as a spread for the table. For spreading on breads, keep soft. Refrigerate for later use.

Great on baked potatoes.

Self Rising Flour ᴷ

4 cups flour, plain
2 tablespoons double-acting baking powder
2 teaspoons salt

Mix all ingredients well. Label and store in covered container. Next time a recipe calls for self-rising flour and you don't have any...you can make your own!

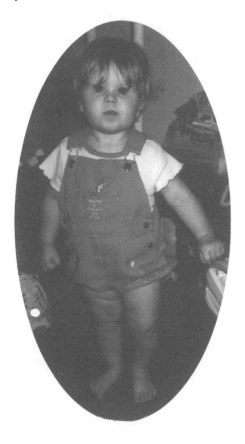

*Granddaughter
Karla*

"Short" Flaky Basic Buttermilk Biscuits *K*

1/3 cups shortening, room temperature
2 cups self-rising flour
¾ cup buttermilk

Step 1: In a mixing bowl, cut shortening into flour with a cutter or pastry blender or two knives until mixture looks like small peas. Add buttermilk, stirring until dry ingredients are moistened.

Step 2: Turn dough out onto a floured cloth and sprinkle with flour. Knead several times. Make a ball and pat or roll out with a rolling pin to ¾-inch thickness. Cut out biscuits with a 2 ½-inch round cutter. Place onto a well-greased baking pan or onto an iron skillet baker. Brush tops with melted butter before baking or just before they brown. Yields 10 to 12 biscuits.

This recipe can also be used for a top crust for fruit cobblers such as peach, blackberry, apple, etc. Add cinnamon sugar over buttered crust.

*Granddaughter
Kristen*

Pizza Dough/Pizza ᵏ

½ teaspoon salt
1 ½ cups plain flour
1/3 cup corn meal
1 tablespoon vegetable oil
½ cup water, lukewarm
1 teaspoon regular active yeast (dissolve yeast in lukewarm water)
¾ cup spaghetti sauce

In a medium bowl, combine flour, corn meal and salt. Make a well in the middle of the flour mixture and add oil and yeast mixture. Mix together. Make a ball and knead on a floured cloth until no longer sticky, about 60 turns. Roll dough into a 10-inch circle. Place onto greased round pizza pan or oblong greased cookie sheet. Brush dough with oil.

Spread sauce over dough to within 1 inch of edge of dough. Top with desired toppings then sprinkle with cheese. Bake at 400° F on medium rack until crust is brown and the cheese bubbles—approximately 12 to 15 minutes.

Suggested toppings are sliced onions, chopped green peppers, sliced pitted ripe black olives, green and sweet pepper rings, ½ pound cooked and drained ground beef, ½ pound cooked and drained Italian sausage, sliced pepperoni, sliced Canadian bacon… or anything else your heart desires!

Mother's Fluffy Rolls

1 cup boiling water
¾ cup sugar
1 cup shortening
1 teaspoon salt
2 eggs, beaten
2 packages yeast
1 cup warm water
5 ½ cups plain sifted flour
Melted butter

Pour boiling water over the first 3 ingredients and cool! Add eggs then yeast that has been dissolved in warm water. Place flour into a large bowl. Pour mixture over flour and beat until elastic like. Cover "dough" and store in a warm place. When dough has doubled in size, then press down. Cover dough well and place dough into refrigerator until ready to use. To bake, grease pan or pans. Roll dough into balls, criss-cross, etc. Let dough stand for 15 minutes at room temperature, then bake at 350° F for 15 – 20 minutes. Just before removing from the oven, brush tops of rolls with melted butter.

Can use recipe to make donuts, donut holes, cinnamon rolls, coffee cake, etc.

"K getting prepared to cook 2001"

Notes:

My paternal grandparents

Grandfather
Hugh McMillan Murdock

Grandmother
Margaret "Starr" Murdock

In memory of...
my paternal grandparents

Hugh McMillan and Margaret Starr Murdock

Hugh McMillan Murdock was born January 17, 1846 in Clinton County, Ohio and died July 14, 1931. Margaret "Starr" Murdock was born November 13, 1856 in Harrisville, West Virginia and died July 9, 1931. Grandfather was forty-five years of age when he married thirty-one year old Margaret Starr. They were married April 27, 1887. He was the son of Robert and Elizabeth Tweed Murdock. She was the daughter of James and Hannah Elizer Ayers Starr.

Grandfather was an educator/teacher in the Cedarville, Ohio area in early life. He inherited his father's love for purity, truth and honesty. He carried out his father's motto from boyhood "If he could not go with as good company as himself he would go alone." His desire of good books— he gave first place to The Bible; and his unusually good memory helped to make his reading profitable. He became a successful businessman, pursuing a livelihood in cattle, sheep and farming in later life.

My grandmother, Margaret Starr was ill with chronic bronchitis for many years. My dad said one could hear her breathe a hundred yards away. Everything known medically was done but to no avail. My grandfather headed south to Waynesboro Landing, Mississippi in 1918 to try a different climate. This climate was very kind to her. She was never bothered with this condition again. The move was quite a transition for all concerned. My grandfather was crippled from arthritis and hobbled around with crutches. They later traveled back to Ohio, selling everything—except household goods, approximately 150 head of registered merino sheep, farm machinery, a few horses and his shepherd sheep dogs, Coco and Tippy Canoe. Two stock cars of the predominant railroad were rented to carry their possessions. My dad told me about a friend Charlie Cooper riding with him in the stock cars with the cattle to feed hay to the cattle along the way. The train stopped in Bowling Green, Kentucky the cattle were taken out of the cars to feed and drink water. Coco and Tippy Canoe herded the cattle back on the train. My dad and his friend almost died from coal smoke inhalation when the train stalled for a time going through a tunnel. Ten of Grandfather's sheep were killed and my grandfather was later reimbursed by the railroad. On they went to Tupelo, Mississippi for more feeding and watering. Finally, they arrived in Waynesboro, Mississippi on October 27, 1918. The sheep and cattle were driven to the farm by the dogs with my dad's guidance. My grandfather and his family lived in Waynesboro until 1921. Then they moved on a three day's journey to Kosciusko, Mississippi about 160 miles away. They camped on the side of the road in order to care for their stock and other possessions. In the olden days there were road thieves. If you left your buggy and possessions most likely there would be nothing left when you returned. Grandfather and grandmother purchased a large farm where they lived until they died five days apart from each other in 1931.

My father tells of his mother cooking delicious foods. Food was something that wasn't scarce in this household. From a long time back, the Murdock ancestors had cellars beneath their homes where they stored fruits and canned goods. Their potatoes were banked beneath the dirt. The remaining part of this large farm today is known as the Moody property located two miles east of Kosciusko on Knots Road. When I visit this property I can't help but reminisce about all the stories that my mother and daddy shared with us through the years concerning the property and the workload my daddy was handed when his father could no longer work the farm. It is to my regret that I never had the chance to know my grandparents except through my parents and other family documents and photographs.

1965 Hamburger Steak & Onion in Gravy *K*

2 pounds lean ground beef
1 teaspoon salt
1 teaspoon black pepper
1 tablespoon Worcestershire sauce
4 tablespoons oil
3 tablespoons flour
3 cups cold water
Salt and pepper to taste
3 medium onions, sliced thin
¼ cup oil
10-inch iron skillet
8-inch iron skillet

In a mixing bowl, combine ground beef, salt, pepper, and Worcestershire sauce. Knead well with hands. Divide into 8 balls pressing down until 1-inch thick round mounds (thick hamburgers). Place burgers into greased skillet and cook until medium brown. Remove from skillet and set aside. Remove hamburger grease from skillet leaving approximately 4 table-spoons. Add flour. Stir mixture with fork until it is a rich brown color. Turn heat to low and add cold water. Stir constantly from bottom of skillet. Add salt, pepper and hamburger steaks. Bring to a boil and simmer.

In second skillet add oil and get oil hot. Add onions, salt and pepper. Reduce heat to medium. Turn mixture over and over until brown. Divide onions evenly over the top of the steaks. Baste each steak with gravy. Simmer 30 minutes or until gravy is slightly thickened. Add more water if needed. Yields 8 servings.

Great when served with creamed potatoes or rice. My husband says this is goooood!

Baked Chicken 𝒦

3 pound chicken, split in half
Seasoning salt
Black pepper
9 x 9 x 1 ½-inch baking dish lined with foil

Preheat oven to 350° F

Place chicken in pan and sprinkle both side with seasoning salt and pepper. Cover and seal with foil. Bake for 45 minutes. Uncover and brown. Remove immediately and serve while hot. Yields 4 servings.

Basic Meat Balls 𝒦

3 pounds ground chuck
3 slices bread, dunked in water and squeezed out
2 medium onions, diced
1 teaspoon salt
½ teaspoon pepper
½ teaspoon red hot sauce
1 teaspoon Worcestershire sauce
1 teaspoon garlic powder
¼ cup ketchup
4-quart saucepan

In a large mixing bowl combine all ingredients. Knead well with your hands and pinch off approximately one tablespoon of meat mixture and roll into a firm ball. Set aside and repeat. After all the meat is rolled into balls, place the balls into the 4-quart saucepan. Pour boiling water over the balls until barely covered and cook gently for 15 minutes or until the red color is gone. Drain water from meatballs. Will freeze well. Yields approximately 60 meatballs.

By using this method of cooking the meatballs and draining the water, you reduce the fat content. Use in spaghetti sauce, sweet and sour sauce, BBQ sauce adding water...the variations are endless.

Barbecue Chicken ᴷ

3 pounds chicken parts
½ teaspoon salt
¼ teaspoon pepper
Butter
1 cup Barbecue Sauce (below)
Baking pan lined with foil
Basting brush

Preheat oven to 350° F

Place washed and dried chicken parts on foil and place into oven. Brush pieces with butter and bake 10 minutes. Remove from oven and brush barbecue sauce on each side. Cover with foil. Repeat with sauce. Bake for 45 minutes. Yields 4 servings.

I usually do two chickens, one to eat and one to freeze. Good for grilling.

Barbecue Chicken Sauce ᴷ

2 heaping tablespoons mayonnaise
2 heaping tablespoons prepared mustard
1 ½ cups ketchup
Juice of 1 lemon
1 tablespoon Worcestershire sauce
½ to 1 cup vinegar
1 teaspoon red hot sauce (suit your taste with more or less)
¼ cup brown sugar

Mix mayonnaise and mustard well. Add ketchup and gradually add rest of ingredients—stirring well until blended.

Barbecue Ribs ᛕ

5 pounds pork or beef ribs, cut up
2 teaspoons salt
Water to cover

Put into a large pot and boil 10 minutes. Remove from water and cool to the touch.

Barbecue Rib Sauce ᛕ

1 cup ketchup
1/3 cup light molasses
2 tablespoons Worcestershire
2 tablespoons apple cider vinegar
1 teaspoon red hot sauce, more or less
½ teaspoon salt
¼ teaspoon black pepper
¼ teaspoon onion powder
½ teaspoon garlic powder

Combine all ingredients and mix well. Hand rub sauce onto ribs and place into a foil-lined baking pan. Bake at 300° F for 30 minutes. Baste with sauce over ribs again if you desire. Remove from oven and cover until ready to serve. Yields 8 servings.

You can charcoal these as well.

*My great niece Rachel Kerley
2 1/2 years old,
Halloween 1992*

Chicken and Dumplings *K*

3 ½-pound chicken fryer, washed, skinned, fat removed and cut into pieces
2 quarts hot water
1 ½ teaspoons salt
1 stick butter
Black pepper to taste

Step 1: In a 6-quart heavy saucepan, combine fryer pieces with salt and water. Bring to a boil, then cover and reduce heat. Let simmer on medium heat until tender. Remove from heat and take chicken out of broth. Cool chicken, then remove chicken meat from bones and set aside.

My dad and Bill
Daddy bought the goat cart for the grandchildren in 1974.
Look whose guiding the cart!

Dumplings

2 cups self-rising flour
½ teaspoon salt
Vegetable shortening, size of an egg
1 cup buttermilk
1 cup milk
1 stick margarine
Black pepper to taste

Step 2: While chicken is cooking prepare your dumplings. In a mixing
bowl add flour, salt, shortening ball (mold into size of an egg) and buttermilk. Knead or work together until well mixed. Turn out on a well-floured
cloth, wax paper or dough board. Turn and press dough into a ball and the
pat out dough with your floured hand. Press until dough is ¼ inch thick.
Cut into strips 1 ½ inches wide with a knife.

Step 3: Bring chicken broth to a rolling boil. Pinch off dough into 2-inch
strips and gently place into broth. Repeat until all strips are used. Boil for
1 minute. Add milk and margarine. Carefully mix with chicken broth. Add
boned chicken and tuck chicken under surface of broth and dumplings.
Sprinkle with pepper to taste. Cool slightly before serving. Yields 8
servings.

*I modified this recipe for today's health by removing the skin and fat and
replacing with margarine to reduce the cholesterol. In the 1800s and
early 1900s, people didn't know that chicken skin and fat was unhealthy
for the body so they left it on the chicken. Some people who are not
health conscious still leave the skin and fat on the chicken today. In old
times, the fat was also removed from the chicken, cooked down, cooled,
removed and used to make pound cakes. Yes, deserts were made from
chicken fat. It tasted good—very rich in flavor!*

Chicken Livers *K*

Salt and pepper
1 pound chicken livers, drained and patted dry
Medium brown bag for coating
¾ cup self-rising flour
1/8 teaspoon pepper
1/8 teaspoon salt
10-inch iron skillet
½ cup vegetable oil, medium hot
Frying screen

Salt and pepper livers lightly. Prick each liver with a fork. Combine flour, pepper and salt in a bag and shake well. Add livers and shake bag back and forth to coat. Have skillet and oil ready for frying. Bring out one liver at time, shake against bag to remove excess flour. Place into oil. Repeat until all livers are in the skillet. Place frying screen over the skillet to help keep oil from splattering out on you. Fry livers for 10 minutes on medium heat turning over and over until brown. Remove from pan. Drain on paper towel. Yields 4 servings.

Sauce for Livers

1 cup ketchup
1 teaspoon Worcestershire sauce
1 teaspoon lemon juice
1/8 teaspoon red hot sauce

Mix.

Chicken Casserole

7-ounce package pasta or rosettes
4 cups cooked chicken
½ pound processed cheese, cubed
3 hardboiled eggs, chopped
1 can cream of mushroom soup
1 can cream of celery soup
1 small onion, chopped
1 pint half & half cream

Mix all ingredients and pour into a 9 x 13-inch greased baking pan. Cover and chill in refrigerator overnight. Next day preheat oven to 350° F and bake covered for 40 minutes. Uncover and bake 20 minutes more.

Chicken Pot Pie $\mathcal{K}$

3 pound chicken, boiled, boned and cup up
2 16-ounce cans mixed vegetables, drained
3 medium potatoes, peeled and cubed
1 10 ½-ounce can cream of chicken soup
2 cups chicken broth
½ teaspoon salt
¼ teaspoon black pepper
2 tablespoons cornstarch
1 cup self-rising flour
1 cup milk
1 stick butter, melted
13 x 9-inch baking dish

Place chicken into baking dish. Place mixed vegetables and potatoes on top of chicken. Mix together cream of chicken soup, chicken broth, salt, pepper and cornstarch. Pour over vegetables. Combine flour, milk and butter. Mix until smooth and spread evenly over the top of pie mixture. Bake at 375° F for 45 minutes or until golden brown. Yields 9 servings.

Chicken-Rice-Mushroom Dish ℋ

10-ounce can cream of chicken soup
3 cups chicken, cooked and diced
1 ½ teaspoons minced onions, optional
½ teaspoon salt
¼ teaspoon black pepper
1 can mushrooms with juice
1 ½ cups frozen mixed vegetables, steamed
3 tablespoons butter, melted
1 cup onion rings, canned (may use more)

In a large mixing bowl combine together soup, chicken, minced onions, salt, pepper and stir well. Add mushrooms, steamed vegetables and butter. Stir to mix. Pour into a well buttered two-quart baking dish and sprinkle onion rings over the entire mixture. Bake at 350° F for 30-35 minutes or until golden brown and bubbly. Yields 6 servings.

This is "Quick" and "Easy".

Chili ℋ

5 pounds ground beef or chuck
2 large onions, finely chopped
4 cloves garlic, finely chopped
½ cup paprika
½ cup chili powder
Salt to taste
Sugar (optional)

Cook meat covered with water. Add onions and garlic cooking until color changes from red to brown. Add paprika, chili powder and salt. Simmer for 2 hours. Great for freezing.

Chuck Wagon Casserole

1 ½ pounds ground chuck
1 large onion, chopped
1 can cream of chicken soup, not diluted
1 can cream of mushroom soup, not diluted
6-ounce medium size egg noodles, cooked until barely tender
15 ½-ounce can whole kernel corn, drained
2-ounce jar pimento, diced
8 ounces sour cream
1 cup fine breadcrumbs, dried out
2 tablespoons melted butter

In a large skillet, add ground chuck and chopped onions, cook over medium heat, and stir until pinkness of meat is gone. Drain and run hot water over meat in a strainer to remove excess fat. Return to skillet and stir in chicken soup, mushroom soup, noodles, corn, pimento, and sour cream. Stir well. Pour into greased 9 x 13-inch baking pan. Place breadcrumbs over entire mixture then pour butter evenly over breadcrumbs. Bake at 350° F or until golden brown. Yields generous servings for 8.

Please double this recipe for larger gatherings!
This also freezes well, except omit putting
breadcrumbs and butter on top until ready to
bake. Serve with a green salad for a
complete meal.

K
Carolyn Murdock Moore
1969

Elsie's Exquisite Crab Quiche

9-inch unbaked deep-dish pie crust, pricked with a fork
1 ½ cups grated cheese
8 slices cooked bacon, crumbled
6-ounce can fancy white crab meat, drained
3 eggs, beaten
1 cup heavy cream
½ cup milk
½ teaspoon salt
¼ teaspoon pepper
½ teaspoon dry mustard

Preheat oven to 375° F

Sprinkle cheese and bacon in piecrust. Blend remaining ingredients and pour into piecrust. Bake for 45 minutes. Cool for 15 minutes before cutting in 6 wedges. Yields 6 servings.

Dad's Chili

1 ¼ pounds ground beef
1 onion, diced
1 quart stewed tomatoes
8-ounce can tomato sauce
2 tablespoons chili powder
2 pound can pinto beans

Brown ground beef and onion. Drain grease. Return to pan. Add remaining ingredients and bring to boil. Reduce heat and simmer for at least 1 hour. Yields 5 servings.

This is Barbara Kerley's father-in-law Ray's recipe. Very good!

Easy Chili K

1 ½ pounds ground lean chuck
14-ounce can tomato sauce
12-ounce can whole tomatoes
1 teaspoon cumin spice
1 teaspoon turmeric spice
2 tablespoons chili powder
1 medium onion, diced

In a large skillet, lightly brown ground chuck. Stir in remaining ingredients and simmer for 1 hour. Yields 4 servings.

Dried Lima Beans and Ham K

1 pound dried lima beans
2 slices ham
        (approx. 1 ½ pounds, fat removed, boned and cut into 3-inch pieces)
½ pod cayenne pepper
Black pepper to taste
1 teaspoon sugar
4-quart heavy cooking pot

Wash beans and soak in water for 3 hours. Drain. Combine beans, ham, cayenne pepper, black pepper and sugar in cooking pot. Cover with water 3 inches above the beans. Bring to a boil then reduce heat and simmer for 45 minutes or until beans are tender. Turn heat up for 3 minutes to boil (this will thicken the liquid). Add salt to taste. Serve plain or over rice. Yields 8-10 generous servings.

I use this same recipe for dried black-eyed peas, 15 bean soup, etc. Add corn bread, onion, a good salad and iced tea and you've got one heck of a meal.

Dutch's Pork Chops & Dumplings

4 large center cut pork chops, lean
¾ teaspoon salt
¼ teaspoon black pepper
Water
½ stick butter, melted

Dumplings

2 cups self-rising flour
½ teaspoon salt
Shortening ball (mold in size of medium egg)
1 cup buttermilk

In a heavy 4-quart saucepan combine pork chops, salt, pepper and water to cover 2 inches above chops. Bring to a boil. Cover and reduce heat and simmer until tender when pierced with a fork. Remove chops leaving broth in saucepan.

Prepare dumplings while chops are cooking. In a mixing bowl combine flour, salt, shortening ball and buttermilk. Knead until well mixed. Turn out onto a generously floured cloth, wax paper or dough board, turning and pressing dough in a ball. Pat out dough with your floured hand—press and flatten dough until ¼-inch thick. Cut into strips 1 ½-inches wide. Bring broth to a rolling boil. Pinch off two-inch strips and gently place into broth. Repeat until all of strips are used. Boil 1 minute. Bone chops and tuck meat under dumplings. Add butter over dumplings. Lightly sprinkle pepper on top.

If dumplings are too thick add ¼ cup milk and gently mix from bottom.

Fresh Quail, Squirrel, Rabbit ^K

Cut up game into desired parts, drain well

Salt and pepper
1 ½ cups flour, self-rising
½ teaspoon salt
¼ teaspoon black pepper
Brown bag
2 tablespoons flour, self-rising
2 cups cold water
Salt and pepper to taste
10-inch iron skillet
1 cup vegetable oil, medium hot

In a brown bag combine flour, salt and pepper. Shake well. Drop game in bag and shake well to coat. Remove game parts one at a time shaking off excess flour. Place in oil and brown on all sides. Remove from oil. Pour off all oil except 4 tablespoons. Combine 2 tablespoons of flour with oil. Use a fork to mix well while it is browning. When mixture reaches a rich dark brown reduce the heat and add water. Bring mixture to a boil, add game and reduce heat. Simmer for 1 hour or until tender. Salt and pepper to taste. Gravy should be slightly thickened. If too thick add a small amount of water.

My husband and family enjoyed the sport of hunting so we always had plenty of game to cook and eat. For frog legs, I do not put in gravy—just fry and serve. To remove blood shot bruising, place game in light salty cold water for 40 minutes and rinse well.

Enchiladas

Greased 9 x 13-inch baking pan
1 pound ground chuck, lean
1 teaspoon soy sauce
1 large onion, chopped
10-ounce can of tomatoes and green chilies, un-drained
8-ounce can tomato sauce
¼ teaspoon chili powder, optional
¼ teaspoon sugar
Salt and pepper to taste
1 cup cottage cheese
¼ teaspoon paprika, optional
1 can green chilies, chopped, optional
10 six-inch flour tortillas
8 ounces shredded Mexican cheese

Step 1: In a large skillet, add ground chuck, soy sauce and onion and cook over medium heat stirring until meat is not pink. Drain and set aside.

Step 2: Place tomatoes, tomato sauce, chili powder, sugar, salt and pepper, cottage cheese and paprika into a blender and blend until smooth. Stir in chopped green chilies, then spoon into a mixing bowl.

Step 3: On flour tortillas, spoon at least 3 tablespoons of beef mixture into the center of each tortilla. Top with several tablespoons of tomato mixture and 4 teaspoons of cheese. Roll up tortillas and place them seam side down into a baking pan in rows of three. Pour remaining tomato mixture over the top and sprinkle with rest of cheese. Bake at 350° F until bubbly, approximately 15 to 20 minutes. Serve with a green garden salad.

Yields 6 servings; can double easily. This is a quick and easy recipe.

Fried Catfish Fillets ℐ

6 catfish fillets, cut in halves
Salt and pepper
2 cups self-rising corn meal
½ teaspoon salt
¼ teaspoon black pepper
2-quart brown bag
Deep fryer with hot oil

Thaw fish in hot water, drain and pat dry with paper towel. Salt and pepper on each side. In a brown bag combine meal, salt and pepper and shake to mix. Add 6 pieces of fish to bag and shake in an up and down motion to coat the fish. Remove 1 piece at a time shaking off excess meal. Drop in hot oil and cook until the fish floats to the top of the oil and is golden brown. Remove, drain and place on paper towel. Repeat process. Yields 12 pieces of fried fish.

This entrée is rated a 10+! Fish is great with my tarter sauce, cold slaw and hushpuppies. Fish oil should be hot to the point of beginning to smoke just prior to placing the first fish into the oil. It works well if you have a basket strainer ready when it is time to remove the fish from the oil.

Tarter Sauce ℐ

1 ¾ cups mayonnaise
¼ cup minced onion
¼ cup chopped dill pickles
1 tablespoon sugar
2 tablespoons dill pickle juice

In 3-cup container, combine all ingredients and blend well. Keep refrigerated until ready to use. Yields 2 ½ cups.

This has many uses: with fish, shrimp, Hush Yo' Mouth Puppies.

Garlic Oil for Grilling *K*

¾ cup virgin olive oil
8 cloves garlic, peeled and crushed

In a one-pint jar, combine oil and garlic. Mix well. Refrigerate several days before using. Yields approximately one pint of garlic oil.

This is used for stovetop or charcoal grilling. The aroma is simply indescribable! Keeps well when refrigerated.

Supreme Fried Oysters *K*

1 dozen raw oysters, water removed
        (lay on paper towels until all water is absorbed)
¼ cup flour, self-rising
½ cup self-rising corn meal
1/8 teaspoon salt and pepper
Oil to deep fry, hot

Combine all dry ingredients in a doubled small grocery sack and shake to mix. Add raw oysters to bag and shake to coat with flour/meal mixture. Take out one at a time and shake off excess coating. Drop in hot deep fryer of oil. Cook until the oysters float. Remove, drain and serve while hot.

Also good! Try this same procedure except dip oysters in buttermilk. Then put dipped oysters into flour/ meal mixture. Shake off excess and deep fry until golden brown and floating on top of oil. I also use the buttermilk method for frying one-inch fresh-cut okra segments, eggplant strips, onion rings, and sliced squash. It's hard to beat!

Grandma's Country Steak and Gravy

2 pounds round steak, tenderized, fat trimmed, cut into 8 servings
Salt and pepper

Coating:
1 ½ cups self-rising flour
¾ teaspoon salt
½ teaspoon pepper
1 brown bag

10-inch iron skillet or Dutch oven
½ cup vegetable oil
3 tablespoons flour
Salt and pepper to taste
3 cups cold water

Add flour, salt and pepper to brown bag and shake to mix well. Add steak and shake to coat. Place oil into skillet and heat to medium hot. Remove each piece of steak and shake off excess flour. Place into hot oil and brown quickly on both sides.

Make gravy by leaving 4 tablespoons of oil in skillet and add flour. Mix oil and flour together with a fork. Brown until mixture is a rich dark brown (not black). Reduce heat to low and add water while stirring. Mix well. Place browned steak into gravy. Bring to boil, reduce heat and simmer in the gravy for 30 minutes or until tender. Salt and pepper the gravy to taste. Yields 8 servings.

Same recipe applies to Stove Top Chuck Roast and Gravy.

Ground Chuck Casserole

2 pounds ground chuck
1 large onion, chopped
1 large bell pepper, chopped
1 large package cream cheese, softened
Salt and pepper to taste
1 large container sour cream, softened
16-ounce can tomato sauce
1 large package egg noodles
Cheddar cheese, grated
Other spices to taste

Step 1: In a skillet on medium heat, brown chuck, onions and pepper. Drain! Add cream cheese, sour cream and tomato sauce.

Step 2: Boil egg noodles until ½ done or limp and drain.

Step 3: Add Step 1 mixture to Step 2 mixture and mix well by folding. Divide into 2 large greased casserole dishes and sprinkle grated cheddar cheese generously onto top of each. Bake at 350° F until done or approximately 20 minutes. Yields servings for a large family of 15.

This is a good main or side dish. For smaller families divide into smaller size casserole dishes. Cook, cool and freeze covered.

Meatballs & Chili Mac ᴷ

6-quart container
16-ounce package large elbow macaroni, cooked according to directions
using 1 tablespoon of vegetable oil (set aside)
3 pounds ground beef
3 slices bread, soaked in water and squeezed out
1 teaspoon salt
½ teaspoon black pepper
4 cups water
4 cups ketchup
1 teaspoon red hot sauce
1 teaspoon seasoning salt
2 medium onions, chopped
1 cup sweet bell pepper, chopped
¼ cup sugar (more or less)
1 teaspoon chili powder
6 slices bacon, fried and crumbled
Water

Step 1: Combine ground beef, bread slices, salt and pepper. Knead together until well blended and smooth. Roll meat mixture into a tablespoon-sized ball and repeat until all the mixture is used.

Step 2: Put the meatballs in a large 4-quart saucepan and add enough water to cover meatballs and cook until the redness of the meat is gone. Drain off the water. Add ketchup, hot sauce, seasoning salt, onions, bell pepper, sugar, chili powder and hot water to cover. Simmer gently for 20 minutes, stirring often. Remove from heat. Drain macaroni and add meatballs, sauce and crumbled bacon. Mix well. Serve warm. Yields 8-10 servings.

If meatball sauce gets too thick add more water. This is a favorite entrée of Charles—he calls it goulash.

Grilled Marinated Steak

1 ½ pounds sirloin steak (¾ inch thick)
3 tablespoons soy sauce
3 tablespoons cider vinegar or fresh lemon juice
2 tablespoons salad oil
2 tablespoons ketchup
1 clove garlic, crushed
2 tablespoons Worcestershire sauce

Combine all ingredients except steaks. Cut steak into 5 portions. Pour mixture over steaks in heavy bag and turn over and over a few times. Refrigerate overnight. Grill your way. Yields 4 servings.

Meatloaf *K*

3 pounds lean ground beef
3 slices bread, dunked in water and squeezed out
2 eggs, beaten
3 medium onions, chopped
½ cup bell pepper, chopped
½ cup ketchup
½ teaspoon salt
½ teaspoon black pepper
1 teaspoon prepared mustard
3 tablespoons Worcestershire sauce
1 tablespoon steak sauce
1 teaspoon red hot sauce
Ketchup for topping

Preheat oven to 300° F. In a large mixing bowl, place all ingredients and knead well with hands until all is smooth. Line an 11 x 7 x 2-inch oblong pan with foil. In the pan divide the meat mixture into 3 loaves shaping 3 inches high. Coat each loaf with ketchup. Cover the top with foil for the first 30 minutes then cook the last 15 minutes uncovered. Yields 3 meat loaves (12 servings).

I usually freeze two of the loaves for later.

Mother's 1910 Calf Liver

1 pound calf liver, lightly hacked with saucer
Flour
1 stick butter
Salt
Pepper
1 onion, sautéed

Flour both sides of liver and shake off excess flour. In a skillet, add 1 stick
of butter and melt on medium heat. Add floured liver and cook on low
heat—turning over and over until done. Salt and pepper to taste. Yields 4
servings.

*The secret to this tasty liver is all in the slow cooking. Liver is full of
blood so the slower cooking seals in the flavor better. Sautéed onions are
delicious with this when served over the top or put into gravy.*

*My dad, James Howard Murdock and
my son, H. Ronald Moore.
Dad was building a den and
had to try out the new fireplace.*

Mother's Salmon Croquettes

15-ounce can pink salmon
1 egg, room temperature, slightly beaten
1 heaping teaspoon flour
1 heaping teaspoon corn meal
1 teaspoon baking powder
½ teaspoon seasoning salt
Black pepper to taste
Oil for frying

Combine salmon in a medium bowl and mash with a fork until all lumps are gone. Add egg and beat well. Add rest of ingredients and mix well. Pour a small amount of oil into a heavy skillet (medium hot) and put one tablespoon of mixture into skillet and pat into a round ¼-inch mound. Fry on medium until golden brown then turn over with a pancake turner. You may have to add additional oil. Brown and remove salmon patty, lifting onto a paper towel. One round of frying should make 5 croquettes. Usually it takes two rounds to complete the recipe. Yields 10 salmon croquettes.

Dutch and Carolyn "𝒦"
1992

Murdock Family's 1930's Beef Hash

5 pounds of beef roast
1 teaspoon salt
½ teaspoon black pepper
5 onions, diced
5 tablespoons ground sage
1 red pepper, ground into flakes
Salt and black pepper to taste

Cook roast with salt and pepper until tender (about one hour on medium heat). Cut into cubes and set aside broth!

Combine beef, onions, sage, red pepper and salt and pepper. Use enough broth to be level with mixture in your pot. Simmer for 30 minutes.

This is wonderful for freezing. Yields about 5 pounds of beef hash. Serve over white rice or creamed potatoes. Beef Hash has been a family favorite since early 1900s. I can remember as a child my mother and daddy canning this in tin cans and using a sealer. This would be done in quantities and stored in the cellar, which is a cool room under your house. You can put cooked rice in the hash. Just don't over cook the rice.

Old Fashion Chicken-N- Dressing $\mathcal{K}$

4 pounds chicken, skinned
4 large onions, sliced
1 teaspoon salt
½ teaspoon black pepper
1 stick melted butter
4 pounds of cornbread crumbs which includes at least 5 homemade biscuits
6 eggs, beaten
2 tablespoons ground sage
3 cups celery, sautéed (or boiled until tender—optional)
Salt and pepper to taste
2 cups raw onion tops

Step 1: In a large cooking pot cook the chicken with onions, salt and black pepper until tender. Remove chicken from the bone and chop into large pieces. Save the broth.

Step 2: In a large pan, combine butter, broth, breadcrumbs and mash together well with clean hands or a potato masher. Add eggs, sage, celery, salt and pepper and mix well. Mixture should be soupy. Fold in onion tops and pour into one extra large greased baking container or several small ones. Place chicken on top of dressing. Slowly dunk or gently press chicken just under the dressing. Bake at 350° F until mixture barely shakes. It will be golden brown.

This recipe also makes turkey and dressing.

Giblet Gravy for Dressing ℋ

1 pint chicken broth
¾ cups chicken liver & gizzards, cooked and chopped
3 eggs, hardboiled and chopped
½ stick butter
Salt and pepper to taste
3 tablespoons flour
1 cup milk

Combine in a saucepan chicken broth, liver, gizzards (chopped), and butter. Mix flour and milk together with hand mixer until smooth. Add flour and milk mixture to saucepan and cook over medium heat until slightly thickened. Remove from heat. Add chopped eggs and 1 scoop of cooked cornbread dressing. Serve over Chicken-N-Dressing.

Chicken-N-Dressing tips: I add butter since I took the skin off the chicken. Greasing the pans prevents hard scrubbing after baking and helps to form a golden crust when baking. The eggs in the giblet gravy must be hardboiled. If gravy is too thin, add more dressing – if too thick add more broth or milk. For cornbread dressing, use recipe for Chicken–N-Dressing except do not put chicken in the dressing. Instead slice the chicken and serve on the side.

Salt Substitution

5 teaspoons onion powder
1 tablespoon garlic powder
1 tablespoon paprika
1 tablespoon dry mustard
1 teaspoon thyme
½ teaspoon white pepper
½ teaspoon celery seed

Combine all ingredients. Place into a shaker container and use like salt.

Oriental Steak with Rice

1 ½ pounds round steak strips
3 tablespoons vegetable oil
½ cup onions, sliced
1 can chicken broth
1 bullion cube, chicken flavored
2 scant tablespoons corn starch
½ chicken broth can water
1 tablespoon kitchen bouquet seasoning
1 ½ cups green pepper strips
1 ½ cups celery strips
½ teaspoon ginger
1 teaspoon soy sauce
Garlic to taste
1 can mushrooms

Brown steak strips in oil. Add onions while browning warm chicken broth and bullion cube. Dissolve cornstarch and about ½ can water and add to broth to thicken. Add liquid to steak. Add seasonings and vegetables approximately 15 to 20 minutes before serving. Serve over rice. Yields 4 servings.

Pappy Murdock's Oven Roast & White Gravy

6 pounds round shoulder roast
½ teaspoon pepper
1 teaspoon salt
Flour to coat
2 large onions, sliced
¼ cup oil
4 cups water
Preheat oven to 350° F
Large Dutch oven or baking dish

Rub salt and pepper into roast and coat with flour. In a Dutch oven, place roast into hot oil! Brown roast on both sides. Place sliced onions on top of roast and add water. Bake in covered Dutch oven for 3 hours or until tender when pricked with a fork. Remove roast from Dutch oven and place into another pan and brown roast and set aside. Yields 12 servings.

White Gravy

Leaving 1 cup of roast drippings in baking pan. Combine in a mixing bowl 4 tablespoons flour, ½ teaspoon salt, ¼ teaspoon pepper and ½ cup water. Blend until smooth. Add 2 cups milk and mix well. Add this mixture to pan drippings and stir until slightly thickened. Remove gravy from pan and place in a serving bowl or gravy boat. This gravy is also great served over pancakes.

Slice roast leftovers and serve on toasted slices of bread covered in gravy. This is called Hot Roast Beef Sandwiches.

Pork Chops-N-Gravy ^K

4 pork chops
¼ teaspoon black pepper
¼ teaspoon salt
3 tablespoons hot oil for frying
2 tablespoons oil for gravy
3 teaspoons flour
2 cups water

Rub salt and pepper into chops and coat with flour. In skillet, place chops into hot oil—brown on both sides. Remove from skillet and set aside. Add oil, flour, and stir with fork until mixture is a dark brown color. Reduce heat to warm and add water. Turn heat to high and add chops. When mixture is boiling again, reduce heat to simmer or low so mixture is just barely bubbling. Cook until mixture is slightly thickened. Add salt and pepper to taste.

Serve over rice, creamed potatoes, etc. with biscuits and other side dishes.

Quick & Easy Grilled Pork Chops ^K

Step 1: Prepare 4 pork chops salted and peppered on each side.

Step 2: In an iron skillet put 1 teaspoon of oil. Get oil hot but not smoking. Place pork chops in hot oil and brown on both sides fast. Reduce the heat to warm. Pour 1 cup of cold water around chops. Turn heat back up until it comes to a boil. Then reduce heat and simmer lightly covered until all of the water has cooked out.

Pot Roast, My Way ᴷ

4 pounds chuck roast
Seasoning salt
Flour to cover meat (plus 3 tablespoons)
¼ cup hot oil (plus 4 tablespoons)
3 cups water (cool)
3 onions, peeled and quartered
4 Irish potatoes, peeled and quartered
7 carrots, cut into 1 ½-inch pieces
1 cup celery, cut in 1 ½ inch strips
3 tablespoons red hot sauce
1 tablespoon Worcestershire sauce
Salt and pepper to taste

Rub roast with seasoning salt well on all sides. Flour roast on all sides and shake off excess.

Place roast in a large skillet, Dutch oven or roaster with ¼ cup of hot oil and brown on all sides then remove. Leave about 4 tablespoons of oil in the Dutch oven.

Add 3 tablespoons of flour. On medium heat allow this to brown to a dark brown stirring around with a fork. Turn down heat or remove from stove and pour in 3 cups of cold water over dark mixture. Turn heat back up on high and add roast back into Dutch oven. Cook for 1 ½ hours covered or until roast is almost tender. Add the remaining ingredients and seasonings. Salt and pepper to taste. Cook 30 minutes more. Remove from heat, carve into sections and serve. Yields 6 – 8 servings

A Dutch oven is a large cast iron cooking pot or kettle with a tight fitting lid. The contents are cooked with the steam made in the nearly airtight pot. This dish also can be cooked in a crock pot—remember to brown the meat and make the gravy before adding to the crock pot. Enjoy!

Quesadillas

1 ½ pounds ground chuck
10-ounce can hot spiced tomato sauce
2 tablespoons lemon juice
1 envelope onion soup mix
Pinch of salt and pepper
½ teaspoon oregano
½ teaspoon chili powder
9 flour tortillas
Butter
Cheddar or mozzarella cheese, grated
Salsa sauce
Sour cream or ranch dressing

Step 1: In skillet on medium heat, fry out fat until pinkness is gone; drain off fat. Wash ground chuck by rinsing with hot water through a strainer (this reduces calories from fat).

Step 2: Put washed ground chuck back in skillet and add tomato sauce, lemon juice, onion soup mix, salt and pepper, oregano, chili powder and simmer until liquid is evaporated. Meat mixture completed for 9 flour tortillas.

Step 3: In skillet on medium heat, melt one-half teaspoon butter. Lightly brown tortillas on each side. Put cheddar or mozzarella cheese on each side of tortilla. Add two tablespoons of meat mixture on one side of tortilla and fold tortilla over to meet other side. In a skillet, brown tortilla on each side to melt the cheese. Top with salsa sauce, then sour cream or ranch dressing on top of the salsa.

Other uses for meat mixture are tacos, burritos and nachos. Yields 9 servings and freezes well!

Roasted Turkey N de Bag ᴷ

Wax paper
16-pound turkey, thawed
Butter
1 teaspoon black pepper
2 teaspoons seasoning salt
2 large onions, quartered
2 cups water
Large roasting pan
1 oven bag, 12 to 24-pound size

Preheat oven to 325° F. Place turkey onto wax paper. Rub butter, pepper, and seasoning salt generously over entire turkey. Place turkey into bag with onions in around turkey. Add water. Follow browning bag instructions for baking. Place in oven and bake 4 to 4 1/2 hours.

For easy carving allow turkey to cool at room temperature for 30 minutes.

Stove Top Steamed Chicken ᴷ

3 pound chicken, split in half
Seasoning salt
Black pepper
3 cups water
10-inch iron skillet

Sprinkle chicken with seasoning salt and pepper on each side. Place in skillet and add water. Bring to a boil and reduce to simmer. Cover with top and simmer for 35 minutes. Test by piercing with a fork into thickest part of chicken. When tender and done, remove from pan immediately. If you like browned chicken, place chicken under broiler until brown. This is great with any side dish. Yields 4 servings.

Simply Delicious Fried Chicken *K*

1 whole chicken fryer, cut up and washed
Salt and black pepper for sprinkling
2 cups flour
1 teaspoon salt
1/8 teaspoon black pepper
Vegetable oil for frying

Step 1: Place chicken into hot water until chicken is hot throughout. Drain thoroughly! Sprinkle salt and black pepper on both sides.

Step 2: In a medium brown grocery bag, combine flour, salt and pepper. Shake well to mix! Drop dark meat of the chicken into bag and shake up and down motion until the chicken is well coated.

Step 3: In a heavy iron skillet pour 1/3 full of good vegetable oil. Let oil get hot, but not smoking.

Step 4: Take 1 piece of chicken out of sack at a time, shaking off excess flour inside sack. Put coated chicken in oil and repeat. Brown chicken on each side. Reduce heat and fry turning frequently for approximately 15 to 20 minutes. Lift out with tongs and drain well. Should be crispy. Repeat for white meat of chicken. The breasts should be cooked about 20 minutes—10 minutes on each side.

You can also deep-fry this! Either way you're a winner!

Stuffed Peppers ᴷ

8 medium green bell peppers
2 ½ pounds ground beef
2 cups tomato juice (reserve 1 cup)
¾ teaspoon salt
¼ teaspoon black pepper
2 cloves garlic, crushed
½ cup uncooked rice
1 medium onion, minced
1 medium green bell pepper, minced
Baking pan with 2-inch sides lined in foil

Preheat oven to 350° F

Wash and core peppers leaving a round hole in top. In a mixing bowl, combine ground beef, ½ tomato juice, salt, pepper, garlic, rice, onion and green pepper. Mix well. Stuff each pepper equally with mixture. Place peppers into baking pan. Baste the meat with remaining tomato sauce. Cover pan with foil and bake for 45 to 50 minutes or until peppers are tender. Remove the foil and let peppers remain in the oven for another 10 minutes or until brown. Yields 8 stuffed peppers.

In order to make peppers stand straight up, crinkle foil and place between each pepper.

Easy Tuna Casserole ᴷ

1 medium package potato chips
12-ounce large can flaked tuna
1 can cream of mushroom soup

Crumble potato chips by pressing bag before opening. Empty flaked tuna into a square 8 ½ x 8 x 3-inch greased casserole dish and add crumbled potato chips and mix well. Pour undiluted soup over the top and brown in a moderate 350° F oven. Serve warm. Yields 4 servings.

Spaghetti & Meat Balls 𝒦

Step 1: Basic Meat Balls

3 pounds ground chuck
3 slices bread, dunked in water and squeezed out
2 medium onions, diced
1 teaspoon salt
½ teaspoon pepper
½ teaspoon red hot sauce
1 teaspoon Worcestershire sauce
1 teaspoon garlic powder
¼ cup ketchup
4-quart saucepan

In a large mixing bowl combine all ingredients. Knead well with your hands and pinch off approximately one tablespoon of meat mixture and roll into a firm ball. Set aside and repeat. After all the meat is rolled into balls place the balls into the 4-quart cooking container. Pour boiling water over the balls until barely covered and cook gently for 15 minutes or until the red color is gone.

Step 2: Pasta

16-ounce package spaghetti plus 1 tablespoon vegetable oil – cook according to directions.

Step 3: Sauce

2 cans (28 ounces each) tomatoes, unsalted
2 cans (6 ounces each) tomato paste, unsalted
4 cups water
2 cups chopped onions
¾ cup fresh parsley, chopped
¼ cup sugar
6 cloves garlic, minced

4 teaspoons basil, chopped
½ teaspoon chili powder
2 teaspoons oregano
1 teaspoon pepper
Salt to taste
Grated Parmesan cheese

In a 6-quart cooking pot, combine all except salt and cheese. Bring to a boil. Reduce heat and simmer for 15 minutes. Remove from heat. Salt to taste. Combine meatballs with sauce and simmer 20 minutes. Combine sauce and meatballs with cooked spaghetti. Mix gently. Serve. Sprinkle Parmesan cheese over spaghetti. Yields 16 generous servings. Freezes well.

Tortilla Round Ups

8-ounce package fat-free cream cheese
½ jar of jalapeno peppers, drained
¼ cup of fat-free refried beans (slightly warmed)
4 fat-free flour tortillas
1 small jar of pimentos, drained
½ jar of green or black olives
1 jar mild salsa

Mix the cream cheese and jalapeno peppers together. Heat the refried beans in the microwave until just warm (approximately 30 seconds). Divide the bean spread into 4 equal parts and spread on a flour tortilla. Next divide the cheese mixture into 4 equal parts and spread ¼ of the mixture on top of the refried beans. Sprinkle the pimentos over the tortilla. Now roll up the tortilla. Set aside to rest. Repeat this 3 more time with the other tortillas. With a bread knife, cut the roll into ½-inch sections and place on dish. Can be dipped in salsa.

Western Baked Potatoes *K*

4 medium baking potatoes
1 pound ground beef
½ cup onion, chopped
1 ¼-ounce package taco seasoning mix
1 cup water
½ cup sliced bell pepper rings
1 cup sour cream
Salsa sauce

Wash potatoes, pat dry and wrap in wax paper. Pierce with a fork on each side. Microwave until tender.

In a skillet, cook ground beef and onion until beef is brown and crumbled. Drain off fat. Put in colander and run hot water over beef to remove excess fat. Put back into skillet and add seasoning mix and water. Reduce heat and simmer for 20 minutes stirring often.

Place potatoes onto the center of a plate and split potato in half lengthwise. Loosen potato with fork. Spoon taco mixture equally over each potato. Top with pepper, salsa sauce, then sour cream. Yields 4 servings.

My Traditional Holiday Dinner

Baked Ham
Baked Turkey
Chicken N Dressing
Giblet Gravy
Candied Cranberries
Ritzy Lime Salad
Fruit Salad
Sweet Potato Casserole
Turnip and Mustard Greens
English Peas
Buttered Turnips
Cornbread
Homemade Rolls
Fresh Coconut Cake
Apple Fruit Cake
Pound Cake
Sweet Potato Chess Pie
Pumpkin Pie
Chocolate Pie
Hawaiian Cream Cheese Pie
Divinity Candy
Buttermilk Fudge
Brownies

This always took weeks to prepare, but a good time was had by all.

Notes:

My maternal grandparents...

Isaac Abner and Minnie Leola "Herring" Herring

In memory of...
my maternal grandparents

Isaac Arnold and
Minnie Leola (Herring) Herring

Isaac Arnold Herring was born February 17, 1869 in Kosciusko, Mississippi and died there December 26, 1955.

Minnie Leola (Herring) Herring was born July 9, 1883 in Vaiden, Mississippi and died December 4, 1957 in Kosciusko, Mississippi. They are buried in Kosciusko City Cemetery in Kosciusko, Mississippi.

My maternal grandfather was the son of Dr. Isaac Arnold Herring. He married my grandmother, Minnie Leola Herring February 8, 1903 (yes, a Herring marrying an unrelated Herring). She was the daughter of John Russell Herring. We called them Papa and Mama Herring. They lived in a large five-bedroom home with a long, wide hallway that went from the front door to the breakfast room. It had a table that looked like the Lord's Supper Table. It was the biggest oblong room I'd ever seen. There was an old wind-up type telephone in the corner of the room. I don't recall ever eating in the dining room.

My grandfather inherited all of his father's property except a small amount of acreage that he left his other son, whom we called Great Uncle George. The location of the property is 3 ½ miles east of downtown Kosciusko on Highway 12 on the right. Grandfather also purchased property on the left side of the highway. Today the Belks own a portion of the Herring Estate. Papa Herring gave land so the Natchez Trace Parkway could be built. This Parkway runs through the center of his property from its origin in Natchez, Mississippi all the way into Tennessee. Papa Herring was a farmer and a businessman. He always wore a white shirt, starched and ironed. I never once saw him dressed any other way. He had tenant houses on his property. He would put up all of the money for the year's crops. When the crops were harvested in the fall, he would pay all the bills and then share the profit with the tenant workers. He was thought to be a fair businessman. He had a molasses mill and used horses to turn the mill in order to squeeze out the juice from the sugar cane. Sorghum and Louisiana ribbon cane molasses were his finished products. As children, we stripped the ripe sugar cane and chewed it until we were sick. As far as I know, Papa Herring never left the state of Mississippi. After raising their family they moved into a smaller home on the front side of their property. The home was built from beautiful knotty pine lumber.

Papa Herring loved to travel by wagon to wet his hook at the river near his home—a place known as Munson's Bottom to this day. Papa's trip to Munson's was later made on foot, but he never turned down a ride if one was offered. He loved to tell of his fishing trips... how many and how big. That is, how many times he had been fishing and how big a time he had! He could entertain anyone with a two-hour yarn of his stories. Then he would start all over again with the same story if you were willing to listen. He also liked to talk about his courtships, then known as suitors. One day as I was driving him around, I asked him if I was going too fast. His reply was "I can go as fast as the car." He never drove an automobile as far as I know.

My grandmother was a tall, stately looking lady. She was well groomed and wore her hair platted in the back and circled. She was a very independent lady and a fine seamstress. I have her pedal-type sewing machine today. She was a great cook who never wanted anyone in the kitchen to wind around her. But she would allow anyone to sit on a stool and watch. Bet you can't guess who got to sit on the stool! Many times I sat on the stool and watched her churn butter. I always wanted to churn the buttermilk for her so I could see the butter come to the surface. Finally, she allowed me to do the churning but after about thirty minutes I was tired of it...I was not allowed to quit until the churning was all finished. Mama Herring would put the butter into wooden molds, work out the water, and cool the butter. Then she turned the butter out onto a round butter dish inherent with a pretty design on top. The butter was used to make cakes, pies, casseroles, and served on biscuits and pancakes, etc. Commercial butter today is just not as tasty as the butter churned at home. Mama Herring was an avid gardener and had large beautiful flowerbeds. Colorful roses were her top priority. She maintained a vegetable garden as well and canned their winter supply of food from it. She raised chickens and had cows that gave them an abundant amount of milk with pure cream—approximately five inches on top of each gallon. I remember she had delicious homegrown tart green apples, pears, figs, crab apples, blackberries, pecans and walnuts. I can still remember sitting under the walnut and pecan trees while cracking and eating the nuts. Her smoke house was always full of home-cured hams, sausage hanging from the ceiling, salt pork in the bin for frying and seasoning the vegetables. The smoke house was always kept locked. She also loved to tat and embroidery and do needle work. Tatting is the art of making a type of lace from thread by looping and knotting thread with a shuttle. Mama held a lot of responsibility since her mother died when she was sixteen and she was the oldest of six children.

Papa and Mama had a well on their back porch. Water was drawn from the well with a pulley, rope and a bucket. This was the best water in the entire community. Later, a new owner filled this well. Papa and Mama had a cistern at the end of the front porch where they kept their milk and other things cold. The cistern was a large, round hole in the ground. It was cemented with stones and part of it was in the ground and the rest above ground. Rainwater would fill the cistern and because most of the cistern was underground, the water would stay rather cool. The things requiring cool temperatures would be lowered into the cistern. I remember a chinaberry tree being nearby... we would play with these berries pretending to make food from them. Some of the children would use them in a slingshot.

I never knew or heard of my grandparents ever being in debt. Each had hearing conditions. I'll always remember the times my grandfather and I went to Vick's Café to eat oysters. He always carried a small coin purse, which I have today. They are greatly missed by the family.

Papa and Mama's children:

George Herring settled in Biloxi, Mississippi but later moved back to Kosciusko. My mother Fannie Meek (Herring) Murdock settled in Kosciusko, Mississippi. Carrie Cornelia (Herring) McClellan settled in D'Iberville (Biloxi), Mississippi. John Russell Herring settled in Kosciusko, Mississippi. Ruth (Herring) Crosby settled in Kosciusko, Mississippi. Isaac Abner Herring settled in Leedsville, Louisianna.

Southern Macaroni & Cheese ᴷ

10-inch casserole dish, greased with butter
8-ounce package large macaroni
1 teaspoon oil
½ cup processed American cheese, cubed
3 eggs, beaten
½ cup butter, melted
2 cups milk
½ cup sharp cheese
Yellow food coloring (optional)

Step 1: 8-ounce package large macaroni. Cook macaroni according to directions but add 1 teaspoon oil to keep from sticking together. Drain and add ½ cup of cubed processed American cheese. Mix well and cool.

Step 2: Add eggs, melted butter, milk,, and sharp cheese. Mix well. Turn into a 10-inch casserole dish (greased for easy cleaning). Bake at 300° F until barely shakes to the touch.

I add a few drops of yellow food coloring to give this a very rich yellow color.

Boiled Corn on the Cob ᴷ

6 ears sweet corn, fresh or frozen
1 teaspoon salt per 2 quarts water
Butter, salt and pepper to taste

Bring water and salt to boil in a medium covered saucepan. Add corn and bring back to a boil. Reduce heat and simmer for 5 minutes. Drain water and rub butter all over corn. Sprinkle with salt and pepper and serve. Yields 6 servings.

We usually put up 500 ears of corn each year from the garden. So this has been an all time favorite of my family for generations.

Best Ever Deep-Fried Okra *K*

3 cups fresh okra, cut into 1-inch pieces
½ cup buttermilk
Deep fryer with basket and hot oil
1 cup corn meal, self-rising
½ cup flour, self-rising
½ teaspoon salt
½ teaspoon black pepper

Combine last four ingredients in a bag and shake well.

Combine okra and buttermilk into a bowl and toss. Lift okra out and place into bag and shake back and forth to coat. Gently lift out okra and place into basket. Shake a couple of times over sink to remove excess dry ingredients from okra. Slowly lower basket of okra into hot oil shaking back and forth twice to separate okra. Fry until a deep golden brown and remove. Drain and place onto paper towel to drain. Yields 6 servings.

I have many compliments on my okra. People are always asking if I'll share the recipe. Doing this my way the okra is very crunchy. Enjoy!

Broccoli, Rice & Cheese Casserole

2 10-ounce packages frozen chopped broccoli
1 stick butter
1 small onion, chopped
8 ounces processed cheese spread
15 ½-ounce can cream of mushroom soup, undiluted
1 ½ cups cooked white rice
2 quart greased casserole dish

Preheat oven to 300° F

Cook broccoli according to directions on package and drain. In a saucepan, melt butter and sauté onion. Stir in cheese spread and soup. Combine rice and broccoli in casserole dish. Pour cheese mixture on top and bake 30 minutes or until bubbly. Yields 8 generous servings.

Brown Rice ᴷ

1 cup long grain rice
1 can onion soup
1 can beef consommé
½ stick butter

In a heavy saucepan, mix all and bring to a boil. On low heat, cover with lid and simmer for 35 minutes. Do not stir. Shake saucepan several times to prevent sticking. Yields 6 servings.

Candied Yams ᴷ

10-inch iron skillet
½ cup sugar (for caramelizing)
2 cups water
4 cups sweet potatoes, quartered and sprinkled with 2 teaspoons lemon juice
1 ¼ cups sugar
½ stick butter
1/8 teaspoon salt
¼ teaspoon cinnamon
1 teaspoon vanilla flavoring

In an iron skillet on simmer place ½ cup sugar to caramelize. DO NOT STIR! When sugar turns to a rich brown syrup turn heat down. Add water and bring mixture to boil until syrup is liquid or dissolved. Add sweet potatoes, sugar, butter, salt, cinnamon and vanilla. Bring to a boil then reduce heat to medium. Continue basting potatoes using a tablespoon until syrup mixture is thickened. Remove from skillet into serving dish. Yields 6-8 servings.

Caramelized Glazed Onions (Side Dish) 𝒦

1 ½ pounds small whole Vidalia onions, peeled
1/3 cup butter
2 tablespoons sugar
½ teaspoon salt
Black pepper to taste

Place all ingredients into a saucepan and cover even with water. Cook at medium heat until tender. Yields 4 servings.

This side dish goes well with just about anything you serve.

Carrot Soufflé Supreme

Makes 2 small or 1 large soufflé

3 pounds carrots, cooked and drained
2 cups sugar
¼ cup flour
1 tablespoon baking powder
¼ teaspoon cinnamon
1 tablespoon vanilla
6 eggs, slightly beaten
2 sticks butter, melted and cooled
Powdered sugar, sprinkled on top

In a blender place cooked carrots. Blend until smooth. Add sugar, flour, baking powder, cinnamon, vanilla, eggs, and butter. Blend well. Pour into generously-greased 9 ½ x 8 ½ x 2 ½-inch casserole dish or dishes (your choice of 2 small dishes or 1 large dish). Bake at 300° F until mixture sets or does not shake (for about 20 minutes). Remove from oven and cool for a few minutes. Dust top with powdered sugar.

Yields 14 servings. Try substituting sweet potatoes for carrots and add ½ teaspoon cinnamon or 2 teaspoons lemon juice.

Charles' Kielbasa Cabbage

1 medium head of cabbage, washed, sliced 1-inch thick
1 teaspoon salt
½ teaspoon black pepper
1 teaspoon sugar
½ stick butter
Water
6-quart cooking pot

In a cooking pot, add cabbage, salt, pepper, sugar and butter. Add water up to 2 inches below the top of the cabbage (the cabbage also has water). Bring to a boil, then cover and cook on medium heat until fork tender.

The less juice the more flavor. Can use 1 ½ cups cut-up ham. I use Kielbasa sausage sliced 1/8-inch thick and boiled for 5 minutes. Drain and add to cabbage as it finishes cooking. May want to fry the Kielbasa in wafer-sized cylinders!

Cheese Sauce ℋ

2 tablespoons butter
4 tablespoons self-rising flour
½ teaspoon black pepper
2 cups milk
½ cup processed cheese, grated
2-quart saucepan

In saucepan, melt butter and add flour and pepper. Stir with a fork to combine. Add milk and mix well. Over medium heat, stir constantly until slightly thickened. Remove from heat and add cheese. Stir until blended. Serve over steamed broccoli and vegetables. Yields 2 ¼ cups.

For white sauce, omit cheese and add salt and white pepper to taste.

Chicken and Rice Casserole

1 cup minute rice, uncooked
1 teaspoon salt
½ cup milk
8 to 10 pieces of uncooked chicken
10 ½-ounce can cream of chicken soup
10 ½-ounce can cream of celery soup
10 ½-ounce can cream of mushroom
1 stick butter
13 x 9 x 2-inch greased baking pan

Spread rice over bottom of pan. Sprinkle with salt and add milk. Lay chicken pieces on top of rice (skin side up) in single layer. In a saucepan, combine the 3 cans of soup, undiluted and add the butter. Heat and stir until butter is melted. Pour over chicken and rice mixture. Cover pan with foil and bake at 275° F approximately 2 hours. Serve warm. Yields 5 servings.

Fresh Purple Hull Peas

1 quart fresh peas
3 slices bacon or salt pork, fried out
Salt to taste
½ teaspoon sugar

In a two-quart cooking pot combine peas, crispy bacon, sugar, fat from bacon or pork and enough water to cover 2 inches above peas. Bring to a boil and reduce heat. Simmer for 30 to 45 minutes or until tender. Sample a little bit of the juice for salt taste. Add more if necessary! Yields 6 servings.

It is best to add salt near completion of cooking. Bacon and salt pork usually have enough seasoning for taste.

Collards ℋ

4 slices salt pork, or 4 slices bacon, or ¼ pound ham (hocks)
1 bunch collards (or mustard greens & turnip greens)
Salt to taste
Small amount of sugar to taste—about 3 pinches

Wash, remove veins and stems from greens and chop them up into 2-inch pieces. Fry salt pork or bacon or ham in a large heavy pot. Reduce heat! Add greens and 1 pint of water. Turn up heat. Turn greens over and over until wilted. Add salt and sugar to taste. Simmer until tender and little juice left in pot. Serve with cornbread—doesn't need much else. Yields 4 servings.

Greens are a good source of iron, potassium and roughage. Cook greens on medium heat in covered pot so you will have all your good vitamins concentrated when water evaporates. If a lot of water is left in the greens you loose vitamins and nutrients unless you drink the pot liquor. Greens reduce in yield 4 to 1 when cooked. I use a deep cast iron skillet or an iron Dutch oven. Turnip greens and mustard greens are delicious when mixed half and half.

To freeze greens in quantity, wash and cut up. Put into a large container and wilt in boiling water. Remove from container and cool. Place into freezer bags and freeze.

Cooked Rice *K*

1 cup uncooked rice, washed
1 ½ cups cold water
½ teaspoon salt
1 teaspoon vegetable oil
1 ½-quart saucepan

In saucepan, combine all ingredients. Bring to a boil and cover. Reduce heat to simmer or low. Shake pot often in order to prevent sticking. Cook until all water is gone, approximately 15 minutes from the time you turn down to simmer. Remove from heat and serve. Yields 4 – 6 servings.

I double this recipe at times to have enough rice left to make rice pudding, one of my husband's favorite desserts. Many people add an additional 2 cups of water. Cook until rice is tender. Drain in a colander. Run hot tap water over rice in colander. Place colander over steaming water to keep hot and moist. South Carolina and Louisiana vegetables and meats are served over a bed of rice.

Creamed Potatoes *K*

6 medium Irish or white potatoes, washed, peeled and quartered
½ teaspoon salt, more or less
1 stick butter, reserving ¼ stick
¾ to 1 cup milk
Pepper to taste
2-quart saucepan

In a saucepan, place potatoes, salt and water even with potatoes. Cover and boil gently until potatoes are just tender when pricked with a fork. Drain. With a hand mixer on medium setting, beat until the potatoes are no longer in quarters. Add butter and milk and beat until creamy and fluffy. Remove from pot and spoon into serving dish. Add remaining butter to center of potatoes, slightly dunked. Sprinkle pepper lightly on top and serve. Serve plain or with gravy. Yields 6 to 8 servings.

Deviled Eggs For Four ᴷ

5 eggs, hardboiled
2 tablespoons sweet relish
1 teaspoon yellow prepared mustard
1 tablespoon finely chopped dill pickles
1 teaspoon chopped pimento pepper (optional)
Salt and pepper to taste
Paprika for garnish

Peel boiled eggs, slice into oblong halves. Remove yokes and save. Mash egg yokes in a mixing bowl. Add sweet relish, mustard, dill pickles, pimento pepper. Salt and pepper to taste. Mix all together well using enough mayonnaise to make it smooth. Spoon egg mixture into and over the entire sliced whites of the egg. Sprinkle lightly with paprika. Can double recipe easily.

French Green Bean Casserole

15-ounce can French cut green beans
1 can French fried onion rings
10 ½-ounce can cream of mushroom soup
½ cup grated cheddar cheese

In a greased casserole dish, alternate layers of drained beans (reserving ¼ cup of bean juice) and onions (reserving ¼ cup for topping). Mix mushroom soup and bean liquid and pour it over the vegetables. Sprinkle with cheese and bake at 350° F for 20 minutes. Remove from oven and sprinkle remainder of onions on top. Bake 5 minutes longer. Remove and serve warm. Yields 5 servings.

Oven-Baked Fresh Corn -- "Five Generations" K

24 ears fresh yellow sweet corn
2 sticks butter (scorched brown) (see note at bottom)
2 cups half & half cream
1 cup milk
3 tablespoons sugar
½ teaspoon salt

Wash and remove silk from corn. Slice off corn with knife twice and scrape to get white milk from cob.

In a large heavily butter-greased 4 to 6-inch deep baking container combine corn mixture, butter, cream combined with milk, sugar, and salt. Bake at 350° F—stirring well every 15 minutes. May need to add more milk the very last 15 minutes. Let stand in the oven, this will turn golden brown. Remove from oven and let stand 15 more minutes before serving.

This dish is worth the time and effort. It is a family favorite for generations. Scorch the butter in skillet to a medium brown as this enhances the taste of the vegetable casserole. Greasing the baking container makes this recipe form a delicious crust on the sides of the casserole. It also prevents the ingredients from sticking on the bottom and makes easy clean up.

Sautéed Onions K

3 tablespoons vegetable oil
3 medium onions, sliced
Salt and pepper to taste

In a skillet of medium hot oil, add onion slices. Reduce heat to simmer and turn often. When onions are limp and golden brown they are ready to serve. Add salt and pepper to taste. Yields 4 servings.

Home Fried Potatoes and Onions K

4 medium white potatoes, peeled, sliced crosswise 1/8-inch thick
Salt and pepper
½ cup vegetable oil, hot
10-inch iron skillet

Sprinkle salt and pepper over potatoes in a bowl and toss. Place potatoes into skillet of hot oil and fry until brown. Remove from heat, drain the oil and leave in skillet.

4 medium onions, sliced
Salt and pepper
4 tablespoons oil, medium hot
8-inch skillet for sautéing or browning

Place onions into skillet, sprinkle with salt and pepper. Turn over and over with pancake turner, reduce heat to simmer. Cover and continue simmering and turning until onions are a golden brown. Lift onions from skillet and place over fried potatoes. Cover and let stand for 5 minutes. Yields 4 servings.

This is a 5-generation family favorite. If you don't care for the onions, omit them!

Irish Potatoes in White Gravy 𝒦

6 large Irish potatoes, washed, peeled & quartered
1 teaspoon salt
1 stick butter
2 cups milk
½ cup flour
Pepper to taste

In a large saucepan, combine quartered potatoes, salt, and enough water to barely cover the potatoes. Cook until just tender.

In the meantime, combine flour and milk in a container for beating. Beat with hand mixer until smooth with no lumps.

Add flour and milk mixture to cooked potatoes. Heat on medium to high until slightly thickened. Add butter and allow mixture to slowly melt. Let stand for 10 minutes. Fold in potatoes and sprinkle pepper on top of thickened potatoes and serve.

This is a long-time family favorite. Can use small new potatoes dug from the garden in the spring and slightly scraped or bought Irish potatoes from the grocery store.

Kristen loves to play with my jewelry.

Mother's Squash Casserole

2 cups cooked squash, drained and mashed
2 eggs, well beaten
½ teaspoon black pepper
¾ stick butter, melted
1 teaspoon salt
½ cup chopped onion
1 cup milk
2 cups biscuit crumbs
Butter, for basting (optional)

Combine all ingredients (except butter)—mix well. Bake in a greased 9 ½ x 8 ½ x 2-inch casserole dish at 375° F for approximately 40 minutes or until brown.

I brush melted butter on top of mixture before baking to make the casserole a golden brown. May also add crushed cracker crumbs to top.

Kristen 1994
1 year old

Grated Sweet Potato Pudding Murdock Family 1945

6 cups raw sweet potatoes, finely grated
2 cups half and half cream (or rich milk)
4 eggs, well beaten
2 tablespoons flour
3 ½ cups sugar
1 ½ teaspoons vanilla flavoring
2 sticks butter, melted
1 teaspoon nutmeg
2 pinches salt (1/4 teaspoon)

In a large mixing bowl combine all ingredients and beat for 1 minute. Pour into a 2-quart butter-greased casserole dish. Bake at 350° F until barely shakes and browned on top. Simply delicious. Yields 10 servings.

Brother/Sister

My maternal Uncle and Aunt
Isaac Herring and "Ruth Herring" Crosby
1992, Kosciusko, Mississippi

Main Dish Stir-Fry Mixed Veggies ^K

2 tablespoons vegetable oil
1 clove garlic, diced
2 carrots, cut into ¼-inch strips
2 stalks celery, cut into 3-inch strips (¼ inch thick)
4 onions, cut into 1-inch pieces
2 squash, cut into strips
1 red and 1 green bell pepper, cut into ¾-inch strips
2 tablespoons soy sauce
1 small can water chestnuts
Salt and pepper to taste

Step 1: In a wok or heavy iron skillet, add oil and garlic and sauté over medium heat until golden brown.

Step 2: Add carrots and celery; stir-fry for several minutes or until partially cooked. Add onions, squash and peppers; stir-fry approximately 3 minutes or until veggies are crisp but tender. Add soy sauce, water chestnuts, salt and pepper to taste. Toss lightly. Yields 6 servings.

2 cups of chicken strips can be used when you add oil and garlic in Step 1. Yields 8 - 9 servings. This is a complete meal.

Pappy Murdock's Glazed Sweet Potatoes

8 medium sweet potatoes
6-quart cooking pot
Salt
1 stick butter
2 cups sugar
1 teaspoon vanilla flavoring (optional)
1/8 teaspoon cinnamon (optional)
9 x 9 x 1 ½-inch square baking pan, greased with butter

Preheat oven to 350° F

Place potatoes into cooking pot with enough water to cover. Bring to a boil and reduce the heat. Gently boil until a fork inserted into the thickest part is tender. With tongs lift potatoes into cold water. Let stand for five minutes. Peel and cut potatoes in half—placing them into baking pan close together. Sprinkle a small amount of salt on potatoes.

Glazing

In a small saucepan, combine butter, sugar, flavoring and cinnamon. Bring to a boil, stirring until sugar dissolves. Spoon over potatoes and place potatoes into oven. Bake at 350° F approximately 1 hour or until golden brown. Yields 8 servings.

My father made this side dish to go with his roast beef and white gravy putting the gravy over the glazed potatoes. This is a family favorite. I had ten people to tell me not to forget to put this recipe in my cookbook.

Pappy Murdock's Purple Top Turnips

6 to 8 medium turnips
½ teaspoon salt
2 tablespoons sugar
¼ cup butter
Water

Peel and quarter turnips. In a medium saucepan, put turnips, salt, sugar and butter. Pour enough water to just cover turnips and cook on medium heat until just tender and still white. If over-cooked they will turn yellow. Yields 4 servings.

At your own risk, use a pressure cooker on 15 pounds pressure and cook for 6 minutes only adding only 1 cup of water. Remove from flame and reduce pressure. Cool down slowly before removing pressure cooker lid and turn turnips out into a serving dish.

My father cooked the best purple top turnips I've ever eaten. They were white in color and slightly sweet in flavor.

Ronald's Doctored Baked Beans

2 large 28-ounce cans prepared baked beans
½ pound sausage, fried out and crumbled
½ pound ground chuck, fried out and crumbled
¼ cup dark brown sugar
¼ cup molasses
¼ cup barbeque sauce
2 tablespoons Worcestershire sauce
Salt and pepper to taste

Mix all together. Pour into a large 9 ½ x 8 ½ x 2 ½-inch buttered dish. Bake at 300° F for 1 hour. Do not dry out. Yields 12 to 15 servings.

Skillet Fried Corn 𝒦

15 ears matured yellow or white corn, washed and silked
1 stick butter
1 teaspoon salt
1 teaspoon sugar
Pepper to taste

Cut corn twice with a sharp knife, then scrape the white milk from the cob. In a heavy 10-inch iron skillet or saucepan combine the corn mixture, butter, salt, and sugar. Simmer until tender, stirring constantly. You may want to add additional water or a little milk to finish cooking. Should be slightly thickened when removing from heat. Will finish thickening while going through the cooling stage. Yields 6 servings.

If corn is not well filled out and doesn't produce enough white milk add 2 tablespoons flour to ¼ cup milk. Blend and add to the mixture. A favorite of my husband!

Sweet Potato Balls 𝒦

4 medium sweet potatoes
½ teaspoon cinnamon
1 teaspoon vanilla
Marshmallows (large)
Cracker crumbs
Pineapple cubes
Oil to deep fry

Wrap potatoes in waxed paper and prick on each side with a fork. Microwave potatoes until tender. Remove skin of potatoes and mash. Add ½ teaspoon cinnamon, 1 teaspoon vanilla. Mix well. Chill thoroughly. Remove from refrigerator. Roll into 6 balls. Make a hole on side of each ball and insert a marshmallow. Patch hole and roll again. Then roll into cracker crumbs and coat well! Deep fry potato ball until golden dark brown. Insert a toothpick that has cube of pineapple and marshmallow on it for garnish.

Southern Fresh String Beans ᴷ

3 pounds fresh green string beans, uncooked
4 slices bacon, salt pork, streak of lean, or ham slices
      (your choice—fried out)
1 teaspoon salt
½ teaspoon sugar

Remove strings from beans and snap off bean into approximately 1 ½-inch lengths. Wash thoroughly! In an iron pot or 3 quart saucepan, fry out 4 slices bacon, salt pork, streak of lean or ham slices (your choice). Add just enough water to cover the beans. Bring all ingredients to boil. Add salt and sugar. Simmer, lightly covered, on low heat for approximately 30 minutes. In the old days, people simmered the beans until the beans are tender and the water is removed from the beans—they begin to shrivel. Sample them and see how you like them! Cooked this way, you have the full flavor of the meat as well as the beans. Yields 6 servings.

Serve with my corn bread. If you like Irish potatoes, cut and quarter 3 medium potatoes. Add potatoes to the beans after 20 minutes of cooking; dunk them under the beans.

Stewed Irish Potatoes with Onions ᴷ

5 large Irish potatoes, washed peeled and quartered
2 large onions, peeled and quartered
½ teaspoon salt
¼ stick butter
Salt and pepper to taste

In a medium saucepan, combine potatoes, onions, salt and enough hot water to barely cover the potatoes. Cook on medium until tender. Turn up heat for 30 seconds in order for starch of potatoes to thicken juice. Remove from heat. Add butter and pepper. Let stand for 5 minutes before serving.

Southern Fried Sweet Potatoes (Side Dish) *K*

Several medium sweet potatoes, peeled
¼ cup oil
Salt for sprinkling

Slice peeled medium sweet potatoes ¼-inch thick.

In an iron skillet put ¼ cup oil. Heat until moderately hot but not smoking. Put slices of potatoes in the oil and fry until edges are brown and potatoes are barely tender in the center when pricked with a fork. Turn potatoes over and brown other side. Remove from skillet! Remove to a brown grocery bag or paper towel and sprinkle a dash of salt on each side. Then sugar while hot. Repeat process until all are done.

These can be deep fried and then sprinkled with salt and sugar while hot. The salt brings out the sweetness in the potato. In early-day frying, brown paper was used to absorb fat or oil. Hog lard was used for cooking. Today lard is practically never used due to high cholesterol content and more health-conscious Americans.

Elsie's Superb Squash Casserole

2 pounds yellow crookneck squash
1 medium onion, chopped
1 teaspoon salt
½ cup sour cream
1 cup grated American cheese (to mix with squash)
2 eggs, beaten
1/8 teaspoon black pepper
1 cup of cream of chicken soup, undiluted
Parmesan cheese (optional)
½ cup grated American cheese (for topping)
1 ¼ cups crumbled round buttery crackers (for topping)
1 greased 10-inch square baking dish

Preheat oven to 350° F

Cook squash with onion and salt until tender using a small amount of water. Drain and combine with sour cream, cheese, eggs, black pepper and chicken soup (optional parmesan cheese). Pour into baking dish and sprinkle with the rest of cheese and crumbled crackers. Bake for approximately 30 minutes or until top is golden brown.

Leftovers are great when warmed in the oven the next day.

Stove Top Sweet Corn Pudding *K*

½ cup flour
2 cups milk
¼ teaspoon salt
3 tablespoons sugar
2 15-ounce cans whole kernel corn
2 15-ounce cans cream-style corn
1 stick butter

Do this ahead of time! Combine flour, milk, salt and sugar together. Beat with hand mixer until smooth and free of lumps. Combine corn in a medium saucepan and bring to a boil for 3 minutes.

Add flour and milk mixture to corn mixture and cook until thickens. Add butter. Let stand for 5 minutes before serving.

This should be sweet so give or take on the sugar to taste. This is one of my favorite quick and easy dishes. This makes my family very happy every time they see this dish being served!

Southern Grated Sweet Potato Bake 𝒦

3 large sweet potatoes, peeled and finely grated
1 teaspoon vanilla
¼ teaspoon cinnamon
½ teaspoon salt
1 cup melted butter
1 cup + 3 teaspoons sugar
1 tablespoon flour
2 tablespoons corn meal
3 eggs, beaten
1 cup half and half cream
(Reserve ½ cup melted butter)

Combine all ingredients and mix well. Pour into a greased 10-inch square baking dish or pan. Pour reserved melted butter on top of mixture. Bake at 400° F for approximately 1 hour or until brown. Yields 10 servings. A family original—this is very rich!

Sweet Potato Pone 𝒦

2 ½ cups raw sweet potatoes, peeled and grated
2 eggs, beaten
2 tablespoons butter, melted
1 tablespoon light brown sugar
1 cup molasses
2 cups milk (or half and half cream)
1 teaspoon ginger
½ teaspoon cinnamon
1 teaspoon vanilla flavoring
1 cup self-rising flour
¼ teaspoon salt

In a mixing bowl combine all ingredients and mix well. Beat 1 minute. Pour mixture into a butter-greased oblong cake pan. Bake at 350° F for 35 minutes. Should not shake when done. Cool and cut into squares. This is great with no topping but better served with whipped cream or ice cream.

Sweet Potato Compote 𝒦

3 cups sweet potatoes, mashed
1 stick butter, melted
½ cup orange juice
½ cup nuts, chopped
¾ cup light brown sugar
1 teaspoon vanilla flavoring
¼ teaspoon salt
3 tablespoons flour

Mix together all ingredients and pour into a greased 10-inch square casserole dish. Bake at 300° F for 30 minutes or until brown. Great when served warm. Freezes well.

Deviled Stuffed Eggs 𝒦

12 hardboiled eggs
¼ cup chopped green olives
1 teaspoon salt
½ teaspoon prepared mustard
½ teaspoon red hot sauce
1 tablespoon dill pickle juice
½ cup sweet pickle relish
Mayonnaise to mix
Paprika for sprinkling
Black pepper for sprinkling

Peel eggs. Cut eggs into halves, lengthwise and place into a large serving dish or egg tray. Remove yolks and place yolks into a mixing bowl. Mash yolks with a fork. Add remaining ingredients except relish and mayonnaise. Blend well. Use enough mayonnaise for the mixture to be smooth, but not runny. Add relish and mix well. Divide mixture back into the 24 egg halves. Sprinkle lightly with black pepper and paprika. Cover and keep refrigerated until ready to serve. Yields 24 deviled egg halves.

For deviled egg sandwiches, use same recipe above except chop and spoon onto bread.

Zucchini Casserole

3 cups zucchini, raw and sliced
4 cups cooked link sausage, slice thinly and crumbled
1 cup instant biscuit mix, dry
½ cup onion, finely chopped
½ cup Parmesan cheese
2 tablespoons parsley
½ teaspoon salt
½ teaspoon oregano
½ teaspoon seasoning salt
Dash of pepper
1 large garlic clove, minced
½ cup vegetable oil
4 eggs, slightly beaten

Butter a 13 x 9 x 2-inch oblong pan. Combine all ingredients together. Spread mixture into the pan and bake approximately 25 minutes at 350° F or until golden brown. Cool for 15 minutes before serving.

Traditional Turnip Greens ⅄

10-inch Dutch oven, medium hot
6 slices bacon or salt pork
1 cup water
4 pounds turnip greens, washed and stemmed
Salt to taste
1 teaspoon sugar
Water

Place meat into Dutch oven and cook out the fat. Add water, turnip greens, and sugar. Bring to boil. Greens will wilt. Turn greens over and over for approximately 5 minutes. Add water 3 inches above greens at this stage. Cook on medium heat until tender (test by a fork being inserted into greens). Taste for salt content. Bacon and salt pork are inclined to have high content of sodium. When greens are cool, cut crosswise with two knives. Yields 5 servings.

If cooked into much water they will loose their flavor.

Sweet Potato Casserole K

Note: Makes 2 medium casseroles or 1 large one

6 cups cooked sweet potatoes, drained and mashed
2 cups sugar
1 cup butter, melted
5 eggs, beaten
2 tablespoons vanilla flavoring
1 cup raisins (white or dark)
1 tall can crushed pineapple, well drained (optional)
1 cup pecans, chopped and toasted in the oven
½ teaspoon salt
1 teaspoon cinnamon (optional)
1 cup frozen coconut, finely grated (optional)
1 teaspoon lemon flavoring (optional)

Mix all thoroughly and pour into 2 buttered 9 ½ x 8 ½ x 2 ½-inch casserole dishes. Bake for 35 minutes at 350° F. Remove from oven. Top with marshmallows and brown or put the following topping on and bake for 10 minutes. Yields 18 servings.

Topping

1 cup dark brown sugar
1 cup chopped walnuts or pecans (dried out in the oven)
1/3 cup flour
1/3 cup butter

Mix together with fork until crumb-like in texture. Sprinkle "crumbs" on top of casserole and bake 10 minutes at 350° F.

Notes:

Notes:

Co-publisher/Editor
My son, Charles R. Moore

Charles is a 1986 graduate of Mississippi State University in Mechanical Engineering. He is employed with Westinghouse Savannah River Company as a senior mechanical engineer. Charles and his family reside at the Midland Valley Country Club's residential area in Graniteville, South Carolina. Charles has assisted me in cooking many of these recipes and has occasionally cooked them for me. On many occasions, he has partaken of the fruit of these recipes. Charles and his brother Ronald gave me the inspiration for publishing a cookbook of our favorite recipes. I know that he can hardly wait to get into the kitchen with his copy of this cookbook to make some of his favorite desserts. He has an incredible sweet tooth!

My husband Dutch
My Greatniece Rachel Kerley

The Big Day at MSU
My son Charles, 1986

"Best Friends" my sons
H. Ronald and Charles Moore
1991

Granddaughter Kristen

My son H. Ronald Moore
2002, North Augusta, South Carolina

My son H. Ronald Moore
1979, 10 years old

My granddaughter Karla Moore
North Augusta, South Carolina

My doctor and friend
Dr. John G. Downer
Lexington, Mississippi

*My son Ronald, his wife, Danna,
their children Kristen and Karla,
2002*

Karla

Kristen

*The Leaders -- my sister Elsie, her husband Douglas
and their son Donald of Aiken, South Carolina*

*The Kerleys -- my niece, Barbara Leader Kerley, her husband Bill
and their children Rachel and Cameron of Aiken, South Carolina*

The Martins: my sister Margaret Murdock, her husband, Hardy Martin, Moss Point, Mississippi, their sons Edward and Murdock with diploma from Yale.

My nephew Murdock Martin and wife Susan Crawford Washington, D.C.

In honor of...

The Martins: my nephew Edward, his wife Lisa and their children Jeffery and Taylor Elizabeth, Lufkin, Texas

Taylor Elizabeth Martin

My brother Hugh M. Murdock's 1931 Model A Ford
I drove this car for 16 years and enjoyed every moment of it. Florence wouldn't sit up
in front with me. Her favorite seat was the rumble seat. My favorite of all cars.

Florence Price -- Write up in book.

Birthday Bash
𝒦 Featured Entertainer
"Dances Of The Century"
Sheraton Hotel, Masters Ballroom
Augusta, Georgia
8-25-1997
(Permission by Sheraton)

The Family Home
Kosciusko, Mississippi

My parents 50th Wedding Anniversary
James Howard and Fannie Meek "Herring" Murdock

My favorite home...

Murdock-Moore Home
Kosciusko, Mississippi

My baking...

My Pride and Joys...

*My brother Hugh
1994*

Charles

H. Ronald

Charles

H. Ronald

My pride and joys... my sons

Charles, 5 years old

H. Ronald, 18 months old

Charles Moore

*Charles Moore
1st Grade*

H. Ronald Moore

H. Ronald, 6 months old

Modeling Sessions and Dances of the Century...

1991

1999

1982

1988

1988

𝒦's vegetables and flowers

My paternal great-grandparents

James and Hannah Elizer "Ayers" Starr

In memory of...
my paternal great-grandparents

James and Hannah Elizer "Ayers" Starr

James Starr was born January 5, 1825 in Indian Creek, Harrisville, West Virginia and died February 25, 1901. Hannah Elizer "Ayers" Starr was born in 1822 and died January 27, 1890. They are buried in Harrisville Cemetery.

My great-grandfather was a carpenter, farmer and businessman. His wife Hannah was a homemaker. My father, James Howard Murdock, spoke well of his grandparents. He learned of his grandparents from his mother, Margaret "Starr" Murdock.

Their children were:

Alphus, November 8, 1854 to October 27, 1876. Never married. Alphus was studying for the ministry. Buried beside his parents in Harrisville Cemetery.

Margaret, November 13, 1856 to July 9, 1931. Married my grandfather Hugh McMillan Murdock. Buried in the Kosciusko City Cemetery.

Sarah L., 1849 to March 2, 1938. Buried in the Harrisburg Cemetery. Sarah never married.

Fannie, 1860 to May 1, 1938. Buried in the Harrisville Cemetery beside her sister Sarah.

Daniel, April 14, 1852 to December 26, 1876. Buried in the Harrisville Cemetery. Daniel married Sarah Nulter December 26, 1876.

The Starr Family starts with Captain Carran Starr, born 1620, in Old Castle, Meath County Ireland, Society of Friends. He had one son John, born in 1645 in Old Castle, Ireland. In 1673, he married a lady named Mary, who was born in 1652 in Ireland. In the generations of The Starr's, they named their children after the generation before them.

My great-aunt Sarah and Fannie inherited part of their father's farm and lived there for a few years. Then sold out and moved to Harrisville where they spent their remaining years. Aunt Sarah had infantile paralysis. The paralysis didn't stop her—she was a schoolteacher and a very good artist. She would paint backward on a glass, The Hills Of West Virginia. Today I have a beautiful painting in my living room, which I will share with you. A gifted lady she was.

My third cousin Bernard Starr of Harrisville, West Virginia has shared stories and pictures from The Starr Family History that he completed several years ago. Bernard's father James Fred and my great-grandfather were brothers. We continue to keep in touch through the years.

Home of James and Hannah Elizer "Ayers" Starr
Indian Creek, West Virginia

Aunt Carrie's Sour Cream Pound Cake

2 sticks butter
3 cups sugar
6 eggs
3 cups plain flour
¼ teaspoon soda
½ teaspoon salt
8 ounces sour cream
1 teaspoon vanilla flavoring

In a large mixing bowl, cream together butter and sugar until light and fluffy. Add eggs one at a time, beating well after each addition. Sift together flour, baking soda and salt. Add alternately with sour cream. Make sure flour is added first and last. Add flavoring and mix. Pour mixture into a well-greased, and floured 10-inch tube cake pan. Bake at 300 to 350° F for approximately 1 hour or until toothpick inserted comes out clean. Leave in pan for 15 minutes before turning out onto a cake plate right side up.

I also love butternut flavoring in this or 1 teaspoon each of vanilla and lemon and ½ teaspoon of almond.

Glaze Topping

1 ½ cups powdered sugar
½ teaspoon butter, softened
1 teaspoon vanilla flavoring
3 tablespoons milk or cream

Mix and spread on hot cake—allowing a little to trickle down the side. Hmmmm good!

Banana Nut Bread Loaves ᴷ

2/3 cup sugar
½ cup butter
1 ½ cups ripe mashed bananas (2 to 3 medium-sized)
2 eggs, beaten
2 cups plain flour
1 cup walnuts, chopped
1 teaspoon vanilla flavoring
1 teaspoon baking powder
½ teaspoon baking soda
½ teaspoon salt

Mix sugar and butter together. Stir in bananas and eggs, mixing well. Stir in remaining ingredients and mix well. Pour into 3 greased and floured loaf pans. Bake at 350° F for 30 minutes or until toothpick inserted into middle of bread comes out clean. Cool in pan for 10 minutes before removing. Turn loaves right side up and sprinkle or dust with powdered sugar. May also serve plain.

This is a good snack or dessert. Serve with coffee or anyway you like. Excellent for people on the run!

*My son and granddaughter
H. Ronald and Kristen Moore
at Father-Daughter Banquet*

Banana Walnut Cake *K*

2 ¼ cups plain flour
1 ¼ cups sugar
1 teaspoon baking powder
1 teaspoon baking soda
1 teaspoon salt
½ cup shortening
2 eggs, beaten
1 cup mashed bananas, (2 medium)
½ cup buttermilk
1 teaspoon vanilla extract
½ cup chopped walnuts, toasted

Sift together flour, sugar, baking powder, baking soda and salt in a large mixing bowl. Make a well in flour mixture and add shortening, eggs and bananas. Blend well at lowest speed of mixer. Add buttermilk and vanilla while blending. Beat well for 1 ½ minutes. Stir in nuts. Pour batter into 2 greased and floured 8-inch layer pans. Bake at 350° F for 30 minutes or until toothpick inserted into center comes out clean. Cool!

Frosting

1 pound powdered sugar
Pinch of salt (1/8 teaspoon)
¼ cup soft butter
1 teaspoon vanilla
½ cup cream
1 cup chopped walnuts

In a mixing bowl, sift sugar and salt together. Make a well in middle of sugar. Add butter and vanilla. Beat gradually in well until all sugar is used. Add cream as needed. Beat until frosting is smooth and reaches spreading consistency. Frost cake layers—top and sides. Press chopped nuts into top and sides of frosting.

Basic Three Layer Cake ᴷ

All ingredients at room temperature:

1 cup butter, margarine, or vegetable shortening
2 cups sugar
4 eggs, large
3 cups plain flour
2 ½ teaspoons baking powder
½ teaspoon salt
1 cup milk
1 teaspoon vanilla flavoring
1 teaspoon butter flavoring

In a large mixing bowl, cream together butter and sugar until light and fluffy. Add eggs one at a time, beating well after each addition. Combine flour, baking powder and salt—sift together. Add alternately with milk, making sure flour is added first and last. Add flavorings and mix well. Pour mixture into three 9-inch well-greased, floured cake pans. Bake at 300 to 350° F for approximately 20 minutes or until a toothpick inserted comes out clean. Leave in pan for 10 minutes before turning out onto a brown paper bag. Cool until ready to stack the layers with your favorite frosting.

Can use any frosting on this cake, but you must try this cake with the Grated Orange Frosting. I normally use my chocolate frosting on this cake – see recipe.

Black Walnut Cake

2 sticks butter
¼ cup shortening
3 cups sugar
5 eggs
3 ½ cups plain flour
1 teaspoon baking soda
¼ teaspoon salt
1 ¼ cups buttermilk
1 tablespoon black walnut flavoring
1 cup black walnuts, chopped

Cream butter, shortening and sugar until light and fluffy. Add eggs one at a time and beat well after each addition. Combine flour, baking soda and salt. Add flour mixture alternately with milk to butter mixture, making sure flour is added first and last. Add flavoring and mix well. Add chopped walnuts and pour into greased and floured cake pan of your choosing. Recipe makes a four-layer cake or a large tube cake (bake for 60-70 minutes). Recipe also makes five loaf-pan cakes (your choice). Bake at 300° F for 20 minutes or until toothpick inserted in the middle of cake comes out clean. Remove from oven and turn right side up on brown paper. Cool.

Frosting

½ stick butter
8 ounces cream cheese, softened
1 box powdered sugar
1 tablespoon black walnut flavoring
¾ cup black walnuts, chopped

Cream butter together with cream cheese. Add powdered sugar and flavoring and mix well. Fold in walnuts. Mix and spread generously on top of each layer, top and sides. Sprinkle nuts on top.

Butternut Pound Cake

All ingredients at room temperature:
3 cups sugar
3 sticks butter
8 ounces cream cheese
6 egg yolks
3 cups plain flour
2 teaspoons butternut flavoring
6 egg whites, beaten until stiff

In a large mixing bowl, cream together sugar, butter and cream cheese.
Add egg yolks one at a time, beating well after each addition. Add cake
flour and butternut flavoring. Mix well. Lastly, fold beaten egg whites into
cake batter. Pour into large greased and floured tube cake pan and bake at
350° F for 1 hour or until cake tested with toothpick inserted in middle of
cake comes out clean. Remove from oven but leave cake in pan for 15
minutes. Remove and turn upright.

*Cake can be glazed or serve plain. Substitute orange flavoring if butter-
nut flavoring is hard to find. Very good.*

Grated Orange Frosting ℋ

1 box powdered sugar, sifted if lumpy
1 cup orange rind pulp
       (grate entire orange on fine side of hand grater except seeds)

Make hole or well in center of sugar. Add orange pulp and mix well.
When layer cakes are cool enough to handle, stack with frosting between
layers, on top and sides.

*As I'm stacking cake layers, I press holes into cake with my knife slanted
in order for frosting to sink into the layers.*

Chocolate Sheet Cake

2 cups sugar
2 cups flour
1 stick margarine
4 tablespoons cocoa
½ cup shortening
1 cup water
½ cup buttermilk
1 teaspoon baking soda
2 eggs slightly beaten
1 teaspoon vanilla flavoring
1 teaspoon cinnamon (optional)

Sift together sugar and flour and set aside. Mix in saucepan: margarine, cocoa, shortening and water. Bring to a rapid boil. Pour over sugar and flour mixture and mix well. Add buttermilk, baking soda, eggs, vanilla and cinnamon. Mix well. Pour into a well greased 11 x 16-inch pan and bake for 20 minutes at 350° F. Before frosting, press 3 slantwise rows into top of cake with a table knife. This allows the frosting to sink into the cake. Frost with Minute Fudge Frosting.

My granddaughter Kristen

Minute Fudge Frosting

2 cups sugar
¼ cup light corn syrup
½ cup milk
½ teaspoon salt
½ cup shortening
2 squares semi-sweet chocolate
1 teaspoon vanilla flavoring
1 cup pecans, chopped

Mix all ingredients in saucepan except vanilla flavoring. Stir over low heat until chocolate and shortening melts. Bring to a full boil—stirring constantly. Boil for 1 minute. Remove from heat and beat until lukewarm (120° F). Stir in vanilla flavoring and continue beating until frosting reaches smooth spreading consistency.

I don't beat frosting too long—I put it on the hot cake. Makes the cake very moist!

Classic Red Devil's Food Cake *K*

½ cup butter, room temperature
4 ounces cream cheese, softened
1 ½ cups sugar
3 eggs
1 ounce red food coloring
2 ¼ cups flour, plain
2 tablespoons cocoa
1 teaspoon baking soda
¼ teaspoon salt
1 cup buttermilk, room temperature
1 teaspoon vanilla flavoring
Preheat oven to 350° F
Three 9-inch round cake pans, greased and floured

In a large mixing bowl, cream butter and cream cheese until light and fluffy. Add sugar until blended. Add eggs one at a time, beating well after each addition. Stir in food coloring. Combine flour, cocoa, soda and salt—sifting once. Add flour mixture alternately with buttermilk, making sure flour is added first and last. Mix well. Stir in vanilla. Pour batter into cake pans. Bake at 350° F for approximately 20 minutes or until a toothpick inserted into middle comes out clean. Remove from oven, allowing to cool in pans for ten minutes. Remove from pans and turn out upside right onto brown paper sack. Cool.

Frosting

8 ounces cream cheese, softened
½ stick butter, room temperature
1 teaspoon vanilla flavoring
1 pound powdered sugar
3 drops yellow food coloring
2 cups pecans or walnuts, chopped

Cream all together except nuts until well-blended. Spread onto layers. Sprinkle each layer with chopped nuts. Repeat. Frost top and sides of cake. Lightly press nuts into top and sides of cake. Keep cake in a cool place until ready to serve.

If possible, I wait three days before serving this cake. This method allows the cake (butter and cream cheese) to mellow.

Aunt Sarah Starr (sitting in the doorway), Cousin Eva "Starr" Patton (left on step), Aunt Fannie Starr (on right step), Alphus Starr (on right without a hat), James Fred Starr -- Bernard Starr's father (lying on ground with hat).

Murdock Family Coconut Layer Cake

Read recipe carefully before making this cake

All ingredients should be room temperature

2 sticks butter
1 stick margarine
3 cups sugar
3 cups plain flour, unsifted unless lumpy
5 large eggs
½ teaspoon baking powder
¼ teaspoon salt
1 cup milk
1 teaspoon vanilla flavoring
1 teaspoon lemon flavoring
½ teaspoon almond flavoring
1 cup of juice (fresh coconut, pineapple or cream of coconut)
Three 9-inch round cake pans, greased and floured

In a large mixing bowl, cream together sugar, butter, and margarine until light and fluffy. Add eggs one at a time, beating well after each addition. Combine flour, baking powder and salt—sift. Add alternately with milk. Make sure flour is added first and last. Add flavorings and mix. Pour mixture into cake pans. Bake at 350° F for approximately 20 minutes or until a toothpick inserted into middle of the layers comes out clean. Remove from oven allowing to stand for 5 minutes. Remove from pans, turning out right side up on a brown paper bag.

With a knife, press slantwise 5 times on each layer. Spoon 4 tablespoons of the juice of your choice onto each layer. Cool.

Divinity Frosting ᴷ

1 ½ cups water
3 cups sugar
4 tablespoons corn syrup
2 egg whites, beaten into peaks
1 teaspoon vanilla flavoring
5 cups fresh or frozen coconut

NOTE: Add a very small about of hot water if divinity hardens too fast. Need to have this ready if this is your first time . . .

In a heavy saucepan, boil sugar, corn syrup and water until stringy when lifted with a spoon or soft ball when dropped into a cup of cold water. While beating egg whites, stream ¼ of boiled mixture into beating egg whites. Continue beating egg whites and put saucepan back on low heat to cook a little more (approximately 1 minute). Slowly add ¼ more of mixture into beating egg whites while cooking syrup a little longer. Then stream the remaining contents of the saucepan into beating egg whites and beat. Quickly, add vanilla flavoring.

Working fast, spread each layer with frosting. Spread and press 1 cup of coconut onto each layer. Repeat until all layers are covered with frosting and coconut. Frost the sides of the cake and press coconut onto sides by holding your hand cupped and pressing. Lightly sprinkle coconut on top layer only. Place cake into a covered container. Keep cool.

If frosting hardens while frosting, add a couple of tablespoons of hot water, mixing well. If frosting hardens on layers, dip your spreading knife into boiling hot water and finish spreading. Even though frosting may be hard, the coconut will soften the frosting within 24 hours. I make this cake approximately 3 days before serving. You'll be proud of this cake and so will your guests. Enjoy!

Candied Fruit Cake

1 pound candied pineapple
1 pound candied cherries
1 pound dates (or fig preserves)
1 pound pecans (or walnuts)
15-ounce box flaked coconut
2 cans condensed milk

Cut or chop fruit and nuts into small pieces. Add coconut and mix well.
Stir in condensed milk—mix well. Spoon mixture into two 10-inch
greased and floured tube pans. Use cut out wax paper for bottom of pan.
Bake at 300° F for 1 hour and 20 minutes. Cool well, wrap in foil and
store in refrigerator. Keeps well, can prepare 2 months ahead of Christmas
or holidays. The longer you keep the better it becomes. A few drops of
brandy over the top enhance the flavor. Slice thin when serving.

*I divide this recipe into many small baking
pans in order to share with friends at
Christmas.*

*Birthday Party
My granddaughter Karla, age 3
2001*

Delicious Harvest Muffins K

All ingredients at room temperature

1 can cherry pie filling
2 cups plain flour
2 teaspoons baking soda
1/8 teaspoon salt
2 eggs, beaten
1 cups sugar
¾ cups oil
2 teaspoons cinnamon
1 teaspoons instant dry coffee
1 cups chopped nuts

In a large mixing bowl, combine all ingredients except nuts. Beat on medium with electric mixer for 2 minutes. Add nuts and stir until well mixed. Spray muffin tins with non-stick cooking spray and fill tins ¾ full of mixture. Bake at 350° F for approximately 12 to 15 minutes or until a toothpick inserted into the middle comes out clean. Remove to wax paper or brown paper bag.

These are great for breakfast or snacks for on the run families. They freeze well. You may also substitute apple pie filling. I give both a high rating for taste and texture.

Devil's Food Chocolate Chip Glazed Cake $\mathcal{K}$

1 Devil's food cake mix
1 teaspoon vanilla flavoring
¾ cup semi-sweet or milk chocolate morsels
1 cup pecans or walnuts, chopped and toasted

Mix cake mix according to directions and add vanilla flavoring. Pour into oblong cake pan sprayed with non-stick cooking spray. Sprinkle chocolate morsels and 1 cup of chopped, toasted, and cooled pecans or walnuts on top of batter and dunk under mixture. Bake at 350° F for 25 minutes or until a toothpick inserted in the middle of the cake comes out clean. Use a knife, press slanted holes into top of cake. Spread glaze over entire hot cake.

I serve this straight out of the pan, cool and cut into squares.

Glaze

2 cups powdered sugar
1 teaspoon butter
1 teaspoon vanilla flavoring
2 drops of food coloring (optional)
Milk or cream (as required)

Mix until smooth. Add just enough milk or cream to make mixture smooth and of a consistency for spreading. Spread glaze over entire cake while hot. Cool and serve.

Dreamy Creamy Glazed Pound Cake ᴷ

All ingredients should be room temperature
3 cups sugar
2 sticks butter
6 eggs, large
3 cups plain flour
1 cup whipping cream
1 teaspoon vanilla flavoring
½ teaspoon almond flavoring
½ teaspoon lemon flavoring

In a large mixing bowl cream sugar and butter until light and fluffy. Add eggs one at a time, beating well after each addition. Mix in flour with whipping cream, making sure to add flour first and last. Add flavorings and mix well. Pour into a 10-inch greased and floured tube pan or four round cake pans. Bake at 300° F for 1 hour for tube pan and 20 minutes for layers or until a toothpick inserted into the middle comes out clean. Let cool for 10 minutes in pan then turn out right side up and glaze while hot or frost when cool with your favorite frosting.

Glaze

1 ½ cups powdered sugar
½ teaspoon soft butter
½ teaspoon vanilla flavoring
Enough milk or cream to make smooth

Mix all ingredients until smooth and pour over top of cake while hot.

Dreamy Lime Gelatin Cake K

All ingredients should be room temperature

½ stick butter
1 cup sugar
2 eggs
1 ½ cups self-rising flour
1 teaspoon vanilla flavoring
½ teaspoon lemon flavoring
3 ½-ounce package lime gelatin

Dump all ingredients into a mixing bowl, except lime gelatin. Beat 2 ½ minutes with mixer. Pour into oblong greased and floured pan and bake at 350° F for 20 minutes or until toothpick inserted in middle comes out clean. Remove from oven and press holes in cake by using a knife slanted sideways. Do three oblong rows.

When the cake is almost done, make lime gelatin according to directions. Pour cool liquid lime gelatin over warm cake. Let cool then refrigerate for at least 3 hours.

Topping

Add 1 teaspoon of vanilla flavoring to 8 ounces of whipped topping and fold. Swirl the whipped topping over cake. Keep refrigerated until ready to serve. Keep leftovers covered and refrigerated.

You may use any flavor of gelatin such as strawberry, cherry or orange, etc. according to your taste!

Ho'Made Chocolate Syrup ᴷ

Used for hot chocolate, chocolate milk, ice cream, sundaes and on cakes as a sauce.

1 ½ cups sugar
1/3 cup + 1 tablespoon cocoa
Dash of salt
¾ cup water
1 teaspoon vanilla flavoring
1 teaspoon butter, softened
4-quart heavy saucepan

Mix sugar, cocoa and salt. Add water and stir. Bring mixture to a boil for three minutes while watching closely. If heat is added too rapidly, the mixture will boil over and make a big mess! When the mixture has boiled for three minutes, remove from heat and stir in vanilla and butter. Allow syrup to cool to room temperature and then keep refrigerated. Yields 1 ½ cups of syrup.

I've made this for my family for forty years. Can use milk instead of water. Very good!

Geneva's Crunchy Apple Cake

2 cups sugar
2 cups self-rising flour
2 eggs
1 cup vegetable oil
1 teaspoon vanilla flavoring
2 teaspoons cinnamon
2 cups apples, chopped
1 cup pecans (or walnuts), toasted & chopped

Mix all ingredients well. Spoon into greased and floured 9 x 13-inch cake pan and bake for 20 minutes at 350° F or until inserted toothpick comes out clean. Cool and cut into squares.

Yum-yum after about three days! I use 3 eggs for delicious pound cake.

Glaze Apple Pound Cake ᛕ

3 eggs
2 cups sugar
1 cup oil
1 teaspoon vanilla flavoring
2 cups self-rising flour, unsifted
2 cups mealy apples, diced
1 cup chopped pecans
1 teaspoon cinnamon
½ cup raisins
2 teaspoons dry instant coffee

Mix first four ingredients together and blend well. Add rest of the ingredients and mix well. Pour into a greased and heavily floured 10-inch tube cake pan. Bake at 275° to 300° F for 1 hour or until inserted toothpick in the middle comes out clean.

Glaze

1 ½ cups powdered sugar
½ teaspoon butter, softened
1 teaspoon vanilla flavoring
1 tablespoon milk (enough to make glaze spread)

Mix ingredients and spread over cake while warm.

This recipe can be used for cup cakes or loaf cakes. Enjoy!

Millionaire Cake *K*

All ingredients at room temperature

1 cup butter, margarine, or vegetable shortening
2 cups sugar
4 eggs, large
3 cups plain flour
2 ½ teaspoons baking powder
½ teaspoon salt
1 cup milk
1 teaspoon vanilla flavoring
1 teaspoon butter flavoring
1 teaspoon pineapple flavoring
Two 13 x 9 ½ x 2 ½-inch oblong pans, greased and floured

In a large mixing bowl, cream together butter and sugar until light and fluffy. Add eggs one at a time, beating well after each addition. Combine flour, baking powder and salt—sift together. Add alternately with milk, making sure flour is added first and last. Add flavorings and mix well. Divide evenly into cake pans. Bake at 300 to 350° F for approximately 20 minutes or until a toothpick inserted comes out clean. Press 3 slantwise rows with a knife down the cakes. While the cakes are hot, pour or spoon 1 ¼ cups of the following mixture over each of the cakes. These cakes are served from the pan.

Mix together:

15-ounce can cream of coconut
14-ounce can sweet condensed milk
1 ¼ cups pineapple juice
Two 8-ounce tubs whipped topping
1 teaspoon vanilla flavoring
4 cups frozen coconut, finely grated

After you've poured an even amount over each cake, allow cake to cool and refrigerate until cold. Remove from the refrigerator and top each cake with an 8-ounce tub of whipped topping that has 1 teaspoon of vanilla flavoring folded in. Sprinkle 2 cups of finely grated, frozen coconut onto the top of each cake and press lightly. Sprinkle more coconut lightly on the cakes. Refrigerate until serving time.

There will be enough coconut-pineapple-milk mixture left over for an additional 2 cakes. This mixture will freeze well. I made four of these cakes for my husband's birthday this year—three were served at the senior center and one for our family. I had many compliments.

Lemon Supreme Cake

1 lemon cake mix
1 cup apricot nectar
½ cup oil
4 eggs

Mix cake mix, oil and nectar together. Add eggs one at a time beating well after each addition. Beat 1 minute. Pour mixture into greased and heavily floured 10-inch tube pan. Bake at 325° F for 1 hour. When cake is done cool in pan for 15 minutes then turn out up right on cake plate and glaze.

Glaze

Mix 1 cup of powdered sugar and juice from one lemon. Spread over warm cake.

Million Dollar Pound Cake ℋ

All ingredients should be room temperature

2 sticks butter
1 stick margarine
3 cups sugar
3 cups plain flour, unsifted unless lumpy
5 large eggs
½ teaspoon baking powder
¼ teaspoon salt
1 cup milk
1 teaspoon vanilla flavoring
1 teaspoon lemon flavoring
½ teaspoon almond flavoring

In a large mixing bowl, cream together sugar, butter, and margarine until light and fluffy. Add eggs one at a time, beating well after each addition. Combine flour, baking powder and salt. Add alternately with milk. Make sure flour is added first and last. Add flavorings and mix. Pour mixture into a well-greased and floured 10-inch tube cake pan. Bake at 300 to 350° F for approximately 1 hour or until toothpick inserted comes out clean. Leave in pan for 15 minutes before turning out onto a serving plate. Then turn over again onto another plate in order for it to be upright.

Glaze while hot with ½ cup powdered sugar, 1 teaspoon margarine, 1 teaspoon vanilla flavoring and enough milk or cream to be creamy. Spread over cake.

For chocolate pound cake add ½ cup cocoa with flour and omit lemon and almond flavoring. I use this recipe for wedding cakes, layer cakes, loaf cakes, sheet cakes, and cupcakes. It's the all occasion cake recipe! It freezes well! I have made approximately 400 of these cakes over the years. Rated a 10+.

Orange Date Nut Cake ᴷ

½ cup flour, for dredging
1 cup chopped pecans
8-ounce package dates, chopped
2 tablespoons grated orange rind
1 cup fresh orange juice
1 ½ cups sugar
2 tablespoons grated orange rind
2 sticks butter
2 cups sugar
4 eggs
3 cups flour
1 teaspoon baking soda
Pinch of salt
1 ¼ cups buttermilk
1 teaspoon vanilla flavoring

Using flour, dredge/coat the pecans, dates and orange rind. Mix orange juice, sugar and orange rind and set aside (will be used as a frosting later).

In a large mixing bowl cream butter and sugar. Add eggs one at a time, beating well after each addition. Mix together flour, baking soda, and salt. Add flour mixture alternately with buttermilk—adding flour first and last. Add vanilla flavoring and stir well. Lastly, add dredged mixture of pecans, dates, and orange rind and stir with spoon several times just enough to mix. Pour into a heavily greased and floured 10-inch tube pan. Bake at 300° F for 1 hour. Check for doneness by inserting a toothpick into the middle of the cake. When the toothpick comes out clean, remove cake from oven. Pour orange juice mixture over the cake while still hot in tube pan. After cake has soaked up the orange juice mixture turn it out right side up. Cool before cutting. Gooood!

Pappy Murdock's Pumpkin Bread

4 cups sugar
1 cup vegetable oil
4 cups pumpkin, cooked
5 cups plain flour
5 teaspoons baking soda
1 teaspoon salt
2 teaspoons cinnamon
1 teaspoon allspice
2 teaspoons vanilla flavoring
8-ounce package dates, chopped
2 cups chopped pecan or walnuts

Mix sugar, cooking oil and pumpkin in a large bowl. Sift flour, soda, cinnamon, salt and allspice together and add to mixture. Add dates, nuts and vanilla and mix well. Divide batter into four greased and floured loaf pans and bake approximately 35 minutes in a preheated 350° F oven. Insert toothpick into middle—if it comes out clean, it is done. Can be baked in other type pans as well. Try using four greased and floured one-pound coffee cans! This is awesome for breakfast or with coffee. After cool, place caps on cans and refrigerate.

I use this as an all-occasion bread for breakfast with coffee, as a snack or I sometimes top this off with whipped cream or ice cream for an excellent desert. It freezes well for months!

Pappy's Favorite Coconut Cake *K*

Make 1 oblong baked "vanilla" cake (leave in oblong sheet pan so it is warm for icing) –you pick the recipe!

Frosting

2 cups sugar
1 cup milk (or cream)
12 ounces frozen coconut, (reserve ½ cup for topping cake)
1 teaspoon vanilla flavoring
½ stick butter

In a heavy saucepan, mix all ingredients together except flavoring and boil for 3 minutes over medium heat—stirring often. Remove from heat. Cool and then add flavoring. Stir until well mixed.

Punch holes in cake and pour hot icing over cake. Sprinkle reserved coconut over the top and serve warm.

I have used pineapple juice in place of milk, adding chopped toasted pecans and chopped cherries. Very good! Pappy's eyes would light up when I served this for desert.

Pineapple Date Nut Loaf

Step 1:

2 ¾ cups plain flour
3 teaspoons baking powder
¼ teaspoons baking soda
¼ teaspoons salt
Sift together dry ingredients.

Step 2:

¾ cup sugar
1/3 cup butter, melted
1 egg, beaten
1/3 cup milk

Step 3:

1 cup crushed pineapple, not drained
8-ounce package pitted dates, chopped
1 cup nuts, chopped

Put #2 mixture into a bowl and beat. Add #3 mixture and beat well then add #1 mixture and beat until well combined.

Preheat oven to 350° F. Divide evenly into four greased and floured 9 x 5 x 3-inch loaf pans. Bake for 25 minutes or until brown and a toothpick inserted comes out clean.

Bread is better the second day after baking. Slice thin and butter or serve with cream cheese as a sandwich filling.

Plain Dump Cake 𝒦

All ingredients should be room temperature

1 stick butter, softened
1 cup sugar
2 eggs
1 ½ cups self-rising flour
1 teaspoon vanilla flavoring
½ teaspoon almond flavoring, optional
½ teaspoon lemon flavoring, optional
9 x 13 x 2-inch pan (sprayed with non-stick baking spray)

Dump all of the ingredients into mixing bowl and beat with electric mixer for 2 ½ minutes, scraping sides down twice. Pour into oblong pan and bake at 350° F for 20 minutes or until toothpick inserted in middle comes out clean. Cool in pan and cut into squares.

I use this recipe for strawberry shortcake; serve it while warm with butter; or you can put a glaze on it. For banana cake mash one banana with a fork and put in bowl, add ½ teaspoon cinnamon and omit lemon and almond flavorings. This is a very easy cake to make.

Poppy Pound Cake *K*

All ingredients should be room temperature

2 sticks butter
1 stick margarine
3 cups sugar
3 cups plain flour, unsifted unless lumpy
5 large eggs
½ teaspoon baking powder
¼ teaspoon salt
1 cup milk
1 teaspoon vanilla flavoring
1 teaspoon lemon flavoring
½ teaspoon almond flavoring
1/3 cup poppy seed

In a large mixing bowl, cream together sugar, butter, and margarine until light and fluffy. Add eggs one at a time, beating well after each addition. Combine flour, baking powder and salt. Add alternately with milk. Make sure flour is added first and last. Add flavorings. Stir in poppy seed. Pour mixture into a well-greased and floured 10-inch tube cake pan. Bake at 300° to 350° F for approximately 1 hour or until toothpick inserted comes out clean. Leave in pan for 15 minutes before turning out onto a serving plate. Then turn over again onto another plate in order for it to be upright.

Glaze while hot with ½ cup powdered sugar, 1 teaspoon margarine, 1 teaspoon vanilla flavoring and enough milk or cream to be creamy. Spread over cake.

Pound Cake *K*

2 cups sugar
2 sticks butter
6 eggs
2 cups plain flour
Dash of salt
½ teaspoon almond flavoring
1 teaspoon vanilla flavoring
½ teaspoon lemon flavoring

Beat sugar and butter together until fluffy. Add 1 egg at a time beating well after each addition. Add dry ingredients and flavorings. Mix well. Pour batter into a heavily greased and floured 10-inch bundt cake pan. Bake for 1 hour at 275° F. Let cake cool for 15 minutes outside of oven before turning cake out of pan.

The secret of this cake is the beating of the eggs well after each addition.

Praline Pound Cake 𝒦

All ingredients should be room temperature

1 cup butter
1 stick margarine
1 pound light brown sugar
5 eggs
3 cups plain flour, unsifted
¼ teaspoon baking soda
½ teaspoon baking powder
¾ cup milk
2 teaspoons vanilla flavoring
2 cups walnuts, chopped
Powdered sugar for dusting after cool, optional

In a large mixing bowl, cream butter, margarine and brown sugar until light and fluffy. Add eggs one at a time, beating well after each addition. Add dry ingredients alternately with milk beating well after each addition. Make sure to add flour first and last. Stir in vanilla and nuts. Pour into a well-greased and floured 10-inch tube pan. Bake at 300° F for approximately 1 ½ hours or until a toothpick inserted into the cake comes out clean. Cool in the pan for 10 minutes before removing. Turn right side up. Cool and store in airtight container.

Prune Cake

All ingredients should be room temperature

2 cups sugar
2 cups flour, plain
1 teaspoon nutmeg
1 teaspoon cinnamon
1 teaspoon salt
1 teaspoon cloves
1 teaspoon baking soda
3 eggs, beaten
1 cup oil
1 cup buttermilk
1 teaspoon vanilla flavoring
1 cup stewed prunes, mashed

Combine dry ingredients. Beat eggs; add to oil, prunes, buttermilk and vanilla. Add dry ingredients to liquid mixture, mixing well. Bake in a greased and floured 10-inch tube pan at 350° F for 1 hour or until tooth-pick inserted in middle comes out clean. Remove from oven and let cool for 10 minutes.

Frosting

½ stick butter
8 ounces cream cheese
1 teaspoon vanilla flavoring
1 box powdered sugar
2 cups pecans, chopped

Cream together butter, cream cheese and vanilla. Add powdered sugar and cream together well. Stir in chopped nuts. Spread on cooled cake.

Pumpkin Cake

All ingredients should be room temperature

1 cup shortening
3 eggs, beaten
16-ounce can pumpkin
1 teaspoon vanilla flavoring
3 cups sugar
3 cups flour
1 teaspoon baking soda
1 teaspoon allspice
1 teaspoon cinnamon
¼ teaspoon salt

Cream shortening, eggs, pumpkin and vanilla flavoring. Mix together dry ingredients and add to creamed mixture. Mix well. Pour into greased and floured 10-inch tube pan and bake at 350° F for 1 hour and 15 minutes. Cool 15 minutes in pan before removing. Turn upright on cake plate, cool and enjoy!

Put a glaze on cake while hot if desired.

Elsie's Tasty Banana Cake

2/3 cup shortening
3 ½ cups plain flour
1 2/3 cups sugar
1 ¼ teaspoons baking powder
1 teaspoon baking soda
1 teaspoon salt
1 ¼ cups bananas, mashed
2/3 cup buttermilk
2 large eggs, slightly beaten
1 teaspoon almond or vanilla flavoring
2/3 cup nuts, chopped (walnuts or pecan)
½ cup golden raisins (optional)
2 greased and floured 9-inch round cake pans

Preheat oven to 350° F

In a large mixing bowl stir shortening to soften. Stir in dry ingredients. Add bananas and half of the buttermilk. Mix until all flour is dampened. Beat vigorously for 2 minutes. Add remaining buttermilk, eggs and the vanilla. Beat for another 2 minutes. Fold in the nuts and raisins. Pour into pans and bake for 30 to 35 minutes or until toothpick inserted comes out clean. Cool before adding frosting. Frost with cream cheese frosting or use your favorite.

Cream Cheese Frosting

½ stick butter
8 ounces cream cheese
1 teaspoon vanilla flavoring
1 box powdered sugar
2 cups pecans, chopped

Cream together butter, cream cheese and vanilla. Add powdered sugar and cream together well. Stir in chopped nuts. Spread on cooled cake.

Elsie's Deluxe Chocolate Rocky Mountain Cake

1 cup butter, room temperature
2 cups sugar
4 egg yolks, beaten
2 chocolate squares, melted and cooled
1 teaspoon baking soda
2 cups plain flour
1 cup sour cream
1 teaspoon vanilla
1 cup chopped walnuts or pecans
1 cup moist coconut
1 cup milk chocolate morsels
4 egg whites, beaten
10-inch tube pan, greased and floured

Preheat oven to 350° F

In a large mixing bowl, cream butter and sugar until light and fluffy. Add egg yolks one at a time, beating well after each addition. Add flour sifted with soda, alternately with sour cream and vanilla. Beat 30 seconds! Add chopped nuts, coconut, chocolate morsels and egg whites. Fold in over and over until added ingredients are not visible. Pour into a tube pan and bake for 1 hour or until a toothpick inserted in center comes out clean. Remove from oven and cool in pan for 15 minutes. Remove from pan turning right side up on cake plate.

This is an excellent, rich cake. Freezes well.

Superb Apple Fruit Cake *K*

Note: This will make three 10-inch tube pan cakes

3 eggs
1 cup brown sugar
1 cup sugar
1 cup oil
2 teaspoons vanilla flavoring
2 cups self-rising flour
2 cups chopped apples (mealy soft type)
1 tablespoon instant dry coffee
3 cups chopped dates
1 cup raisins
2 teaspoons cinnamon
½ teaspoon cloves
1 pound candied red cherries
1 pound candied green cherries
1 pound candied pineapple
1 quart pecans or walnuts, chopped

Note: Sprinkle 1 cup of flour over candied fruit mixture and toss.

In a large mixing bowl, combine eggs, sugars, oil and vanilla flavoring. Beat until smooth. Add rest of ingredients. Using gloves, mix with your hands until well coated. Place mixture into heavily greased and floured tube pans. Bake at 275° F for approximately 1 hour and 15 minutes or until a toothpick inserted in the middle comes out clean. Remove from oven and cool 15 minutes in pan. Remove and turn upright. Use one cake plate to turn out onto and another to turn upright.

You may want to use bundt or loaf pans or smaller pans to use as Christmas gifts. Adjust accordingly. Very moist.

Heavenly Carrot Cake ᴷ

2 cups sugar
1 ½ cups oil
1 teaspoon vanilla flavoring
4 eggs, beaten
2 cups plain flour
2 teaspoons baking soda
2 teaspoons cinnamon
½ teaspoon salt
2 cups finely grated carrots
      (grate on hand grater on fine side)
1 cup pecans (or walnuts), toasted
      (reserve ¼ cup for topping)

In a large mixing bowl, mix together sugar, oil, and vanilla flavoring. Add beaten eggs. Mix until blended. Sift together flour, baking soda, cinnamon and salt. Add dry mixture to liquid mixture and mix well. Gradually add finely-grated carrots and nuts mixing well. Pour into three 8 or 9-inch greased and floured cake pans. Bake at 350° F for 15 to 20 minutes or until toothpick inserted into the middle comes out clean. Remove from oven and let stand for 10 minutes. Loosen around the sides of pan with a knife. Turn out onto brown grocery bag up right and cool!

Frosting

1 pound box powdered sugar
8 ounces cream cheese, softened
½ stick butter, room temperature
2 teaspoons vanilla flavoring
1 cup pecans (or walnuts), chopped & toasted

Combine all ingredients (except nuts). Mix well and spread between layers, on top and sides. Sprinkle chopped nuts on top.

Strawberry Cake

5-ounce package strawberries, frozen & crushed
3 ½-ounce package strawberry gelatin
1 cup vegetable oil
4 eggs
1 white cake mix
2 tablespoons self-rising flour
¾ cup water

Mix strawberries and gelatin with oil and eggs. Beat well. Add water, cake mix and flour. Beat for 2 minutes. Pour into four round 8-inch greased and floured layer pans. Bake at 350° F until layers spring back when touched in the middle.

Fruit Frosting

1 box powdered sugar
5-ounce package strawberries, drained and crushed
½ stick butter, room temperature

Mix all together and spread on cool layers. Refrigerate for a few hours then serve.

Three Layer Banana Cream Cake ℑ

1 white cake mix
3 eggs
1 ¼ cups buttermilk
1/3 cup oil
1 teaspoon cinnamon
2 teaspoons vanilla flavoring
2 bananas, mashed well
1 cup chopped walnuts
¼ cup chopped walnuts, for garnish

Combine cake mix and all other ingredients together except nuts. Mix well for 2 minutes at high speed. Stir in nuts. Pour into well-greased and floured pans. Bake at 350° F for 20 to 25 minutes or until toothpick inserted into cake middle comes out clean. Remove from oven. Turn out layers upside right on brown paper. Cool and stack layers with frosting in between on top and sides. Garnish with remaining nuts.

Frosting

Mix together:

1 box powdered sugar
8 ounces cream cheese
½ stick butter
Dash of salt
1 cup walnuts, chopped

Makes enough to frost 2 sheet cakes or one three-layer cake.

Three Layer Stack Cake

First Layer:

1 cup plain flour
1 tablespoon sugar
1 stick butter, room temperature
½ cup chopped pecans

Mix until dough is formed and press dough into 9 x 13-inch oblong pan. Bake at 350° F for 15 minutes.

Second Layer:

8 ounces cream cheese, room temperature
1 cup powdered sugar
16 ounces whipped topping
1 teaspoon vanilla flavoring

Cream cheese and sugar together. Fold in whipped topping and vanilla flavoring. Spread on cooled crust.

Third Layer:

2 small boxes instant chocolate pudding
3 cups cold milk
1 teaspoon vanilla flavoring
16 ounces whipped topping
1 cup pecans, oven toasted, chopped and cooled

Mix all ingredients (except whipped topping and pecans) and beat until smooth. Chill and then spread on top of second layer. Top as heavily as desired with whipped topping. Add or sprinkle pecans that have been toasted in oven and cooled. Chill and then cut into small squares.

Very good. Very rich. Rated 10+.

Two Layer Orange Cake 𝒦

1 yellow cake mix
1 package instant vanilla pudding
½ cup oil
4 eggs
1 cup buttermilk

Mix all ingredients in a large mixing bowl and beat well. Pour into two greased and floured 9-inch cake layer pans and bake at 350° F for 20 minutes or until a toothpick inserted into the cake comes out clean. While cake is still warm punch holes in layers while stacking and put the following frosting on layer, top and sides. Serve warm or cool...good either way!

Frosting

1 box powdered sugar
2 oranges (grate whole orange on fine side of hand grater, except seeds)

Mix together and blend well. Spread on warm layers.

Store leftover frosting in refrigerator for your next cake or freeze for later. Crushed pineapple can be substituted for oranges.

White Cake Supreme

All ingredients should be room temperature

¾ cup vegetable shortening
1 ½ cups sugar
1 ½ teaspoons vanilla
2 ¼ cups plain flour, sifted
3 teaspoons baking powder
½ teaspoon salt
1 cup milk
5 egg whites, stiffly beaten

Cream shortening and sugar well until fluffy. Add vanilla and mix well. Sift together flour, baking powder and salt. Add to creamed mixture alternately with milk, beating well after each addition. Gently fold in beaten egg whites. Bake in two greased and floured 9-inch cake pans for 20 minutes at 375° F. Cool in pans for ten minutes before removing.

This cake is a moist, fine textured cake. Any frosting can be used such as fresh coconut, caramel, chocolate, orange, pineapple, strawberry, etc. I'm proud to have this recipe.

Cheesecake

10-inch spring form cake pan, greased

Crust:

1 ¼ cups graham cracker crumbs
2 teaspoons sugar
½ stick butter, room temperature

In a mixing bowl, mix above ingredients and press into cake pan. Allow 1 inch on sides of pan.

Filling:

4 8-ounce packages cream cheese, room temperature
1 ¼ cups sugar
4 large eggs, slightly beaten
1 teaspoon vanilla flavoring
2 tablespoons corn starch
½ cup lemon juice
1 cup sour cream, room temperature

Preheat oven to 400° F. In a large mixing bowl, combine cream cheese and sugar. Beat until smooth. Add eggs, vanilla, cornstarch and lemon juice. Beat until well blended. Fold in sour cream. Spoon mixture over graham cracker crumbs mixture into cake pan. Bake 10 minutes. Reduce oven heat to 200° F and bake 1 hour 15 minutes or until a knife inserted in center comes out clean. Cool in pan.

Topping can be blueberry, strawberry or cherry pie filling. I love pineapple. Try my pineapple glaze topping.

Coconut Cake

1 yellow cake mix

Bake according to directions for two layers. Split each layer into halves to make four layers total.

Icing

12 ounces coconut, frozen
8 ounces sour cream, room temperature
1 ½ cups sugar
1 ½ cups whipped topping
1 teaspoon vanilla flavoring
1 cup coconut, frozen & finely grated

Mix coconut, sour cream, and sugar together. Spread this mixture between each layer, but reserve about 1 cup of this mixture and spread this onto top of cake. Fold vanilla into the 1 ½ cups of whipped topping and spread over top of cake. Sprinkle top of cake with coconut.

Divinity Candy or Frosting
For 4-Layer Cake ꝗ

3 cups sugar
4 tablespoons corn syrup
1 ½ cups water
2 egg whites, beaten into peaks
1 teaspoon vanilla flavoring

Note: Add a very small about of hot water if divinity hardens too fast.
Need to have this ready if this is your first time . . .

In a heavy saucepan, boil sugar, corn syrup and water until stringy when
lifted with a spoon or soft ball when dropped into a cup of cold water.
While beating egg whites, stream ¼ of boiled mixture into beating egg
whites. Continue beating egg whites and put saucepan back on low heat to
cook a little more (approximately 1 minute). Slowly add ¼ more of
mixture into beating egg whites while cooking syrup a little longer. Then
stream the remaining contents of the saucepan into beating egg whites and
beat. Quickly, add vanilla flavoring. When the egg whites lose their gloss,
quit beating. Quickly spoon onto wax paper by teaspoonfuls using another
spoon to help remove from original teaspoon. Allow divinity to dry on
wax paper before storing in cookie tins (no plastic ware).

*I use divinity frosting on my Million Dollar Pound Cake recipe, dividing
the mixture for four 9-inch layers. I press slant-wise holes into the cake
layers with a knife. Before frosting I put coconut juice, pineapple juice or
cream of coconut on cake layers. If the frosting hardens too quickly, dip
knife in a glass of hot water and smooth out icing on your cake. Add
finely-grated coconut to the top of each layer if making a coconut cake. I
prefer to use fresh coconut—it's more trouble, but this is a family favorite
and worth the effort! Only use glass or stainless mixing bowls-very
important!*

Orange-Pineapple Cake

1 pineapple cake mix
½ cup vegetable oil
4 eggs
2/3 cup mandarin oranges (juice and pulp)

Mix all together and beat for 2 minutes. Divide mixture into four 8-inch round greased and floured cake pans. Bake at 350° F for 15 minutes or until a toothpick comes out clean when inserted into the middle of the cake.

Frosting

Makes enough for two cakes:

1 small box instant vanilla pudding
2 cups crushed pineapple, juice and pulp
16 ounces whipped topping

Mix dry pudding mix with pineapple and juice. Fold in whipped topping. Refrigerate. Have cold before spreading on cake layers. Cover 4 layers well, then do sides. Keep cake covered in refrigerator 4 days before serving. Moist!!!!!

Goodie Squares

Step 1: Mix together

1 yellow cake mix
1 stick butter (or margarine)
1 egg

Mix will be stiff. Pat into greased and floured 9 x 13-inch oblong pan.

Step 2: Beat with a hand mixer on high for 2 minutes

3 eggs
8 ounces cream cheese, softened
1 box powdered sugar
1 teaspoon vanilla flavoring

Pour over the first part. Bake at 350° F for 35 to 40 minutes. Cool before cutting into small squares. Very good!

Three Layer Chocolate Cake *K*

All ingredients should be room temperature

2 sticks butter
1 stick margarine
3 cups sugar
3 cups plain flour, unsifted unless lumpy
5 large eggs
½ teaspoon baking powder
¼ teaspoon salt
1 cup milk
1 teaspoon vanilla flavoring
1 teaspoon lemon flavoring
½ teaspoon almond flavoring

In a large mixing bowl, cream together sugar, butter, and margarine until light and fluffy. Add eggs one at a time, beating well after each addition. Combine flour, baking powder and salt. Add alternately with milk. Make sure flour is added first and last. Add flavorings. Pour mixture into three well-greased and floured 9-inch cake pans. Bake at 300 to 350° F for approximately 20 minutes or until toothpick inserted comes out clean. Leave in pans for 10 minutes before turning out onto a brown paper bag. Cool.

Chocolate Frosting

3 cups sugar
¾ cup cocoa
Dash of salt
1 ½ cups milk or half & half cream
½ stick butter
2 teaspoons vanilla flavoring
1 cup walnuts, chopped (for topping)

In a large heavy saucepan, combine sugar, cocoa and salt. Add milk and stir while cooking on high heat until mixture comes to a rolling boil. Reduce heat and cook until a hard ball forms when dropped into a cup of cold water. Remove from heat. Add butter and flavoring. Mix well. Beat until the mixture thickens (will thicken as mixture cools). Have first layer of cake on plate. Frost between the layers of cake, on the top and the sides. If frosting gets too hard insert a knife into boiling hot water and spread out frosting. Press walnuts into frosting on top layer.

My son Ronald
2002

German Chocolate Layer Cake

2 sticks butter, room temperature
2 cups sugar
4 egg yolks
4-ounce bar sweet German chocolate, melted
1 teaspoon vanilla flavoring
2 cups plain flour
1 teaspoon baking soda
½ teaspoon cinnamon
¼ teaspoon salt
1 cup buttermilk
4 egg whites, stiffly beaten
3 greased and floured 9-inch round cake pans

In a mixing bowl, cream the butter and sugar until light and fluffy. Add the egg yolks, one at a time, beating well after each addition. Add chocolate and vanilla and mix well. Sift together flour, baking soda, cinnamon and salt and add to batter alternating with milk and beating after each addition. Make sure flour mixture is added first and last. Fold in egg whites gently. Pour into cake pans and bake at 350° F for 30 to 40 minutes or until toothpick inserted into middle comes out clean. Remove from oven and cool 5 minutes. Turn out right side up on brown paper bag and cool before frosting. Frost with Coconut-Pecan Frosting.

Coconut-Pecan Frosting

1 ½ cups evaporated milk (12-ounce can)
1 ½ cups sugar
4 egg yolks, beaten
1 ½ sticks butter
1 ½ teaspoons vanilla flavoring
2 cups coconut, flaked
1 ½ cups walnuts or pecans, chopped

In a saucepan, combine milk, sugar, egg yolks, butter and flavoring. Mix well. Cook over medium heat stirring constantly until mixture thickens. Remove from heat and stir in coconut and nuts. Mix well and frost between the cake layers, top and sides. Yields 4 1/3 cups frosting.

This has been a family favorite for many years. I've made this recipe using a tube pan for baking and halving the frosting recipe...great either way!

Cream Cheese Frosting

1 pound box of powdered sugar, sifted
8 ounces cream cheese, softened
½ stick butter, softened
1 teaspoon vanilla flavoring
Cream or milk (approximately 3 tablespoons, more or less)
1 cup pecans, chopped and toasted

In a large mixing bowl sift powdered sugar. Make a well or hole in the middle of sugar. Add cream cheese, butter and vanilla. Place an electric hand mixer into the well and mix on low. Mix until powdered sugar is blended into a ball. Add cream until mixture is of spreading consistency. Fold in nuts. Frosting is ready for stacking cake layers. Frost between layers, top and sides generously. If any mixture is left over refrigerate or freeze. Yields frosting for 3 layers.

Grated Orange Frosting

1 box powdered sugar, sifted if lumpy
1 cup orange rind pulp
      (grate entire orange on fine side of hand grater except seeds)

Make hole or well in center of sugar. Mix well. When layer cakes are cool enough to handle, stack them with frosting between layers, on top and sides.

As I'm stacking cake layers, I press holes into cake with my knife slanted in order for frosting to sink into the layers.

All Occasion Custard Sauce *K*

3 eggs
2/3 cup sugar
2 tablespoons flour
Pinch of salt
1 quart milk
1 teaspoon vanilla flavoring

In a medium size mixing bowl beat eggs. Add sugar and beat until well blended. Add flour and salt. Mix well.

Heat milk in a heavy saucepan adding egg mixture. Cook over low heat until slightly thickened. Continue stirring until cool to prevent scorching! Add vanilla flavoring. Cool and keep chilled until ready to serve! Yields 5 ½ cups.

This sauce is used in a variety of ways such as cake toppings and banana pudding. Mix in a sprinkle of nutmeg and serve chilled in a custard cup.

All Occasion Decorating Frosting ᴷ

1 pound box powdered sugar
¼ cup water
½ cup shortening
1/8 teaspoon salt
1 teaspoon vanilla flavoring
1 teaspoon butter flavoring
Food coloring of choice

Mix all together, beating well. Can use this as a frosting for decorating all occasion cakes such as birthday, wedding or writing (decorating). Store in refrigerator for several weeks, — works better if being used for writing on a cake. Can divide and make many colors in small quantities.

Caramel Frosting

2 cups brown sugar
½ cup milk
½ cup butter
1/8 teaspoon salt
1 teaspoon vanilla

Combine sugar, milk, butter and salt. Mix well. Bring to a boil slowly. Stir until it boils, but don't stir while boiling. Boil for 3 minutes. Remove from heat and add vanilla. Cool for about 10 minutes. Pour into small mixing bowl, and beat at high speed until spreading consistency. Yields 2 ¼ cups icing for a two layer 9-inch cake.

Caramel-Coconut-Pecan Frosting 𝒦

2 cups sugar
2 cups milk (or half and half)
1 tablespoon corn syrup
2 cups (12 ounces) grated coconut, frozen
2 tablespoons caramelized sugar syrup (see my recipe)
2 teaspoons vanilla
½ stick butter
1 cup pecans, chopped and toasted pecans

In a large heavy saucepan combine all ingredients except pecans. Bring to a boil. Continue to cook over medium heat for 5 minutes and cool. Add nuts. Makes enough frosting for a three-layer cake or 2 oblong cakes.

Chocolate Fudge 𝒦

3 cups sugar
¾ cup cocoa
Dash of salt
1 ½ cups milk
½ stick butter
2 teaspoons vanilla flavoring
1 cup nuts, chopped

Step 1: Combine sugar, cocoa and salt. Add milk and mix well.

Step 2: In a large heavy saucepan put Step 1 ingredients. Cook on high heat until this mixture comes to a rolling boil. Reduce heat and boil until a hard ball forms when dropped into cold water. Remove from heat and add butter and vanilla flavoring. Mix well. Add nuts and beat until thickened. Will thicken more as the mixture cools. Pour into greased platter, cool and cut into small squares. When completely cold on both sides, store in airtight container.

I have made this since I was very young. Good!

Coconut-Pecan Frosting

1 cup evaporated milk
1 cup sugar
3 egg yolks, slightly beaten
½ cup butter
1 teaspoon vanilla
1 ½ cups flaked coconut, or frozen
1 cup chopped pecans, or walnuts

Combine first four ingredients in a saucepan. Cook and stir over medium heat until thickened (about 10 to 13 minutes). Stir in the vanilla, coconut and nuts. Cool until thick enough to spread, beating occasionally. Yields 2 ½ cups frosting.

I use this frosting for my German Chocolate, apple, and fruit cocktail cakes.

Fudge Frosting

1 stick butter, room temperature
4 tablespoons cocoa
6 tablespoons milk (or cream)
1-pound box powdered sugar
1 teaspoon vanilla
1 cup chopped nuts

Combine butter, cocoa and milk and cook over low heat until butter melts. Stir in powdered sugar, vanilla and chopped nuts. Beat for 2 minutes. Spread on hot cake. Fast and easy!

Lemon Sauce *K*

1 ½ cups sugar
4 tablespoons cornstarch
1/8 teaspoon salt
1 ¼ cups water
2 egg yolks, beaten
6 tablespoons lemon juice
2 teaspoons lemon peel, finely grated
2 tablespoons butter

In a heavy saucepan mix sugar, cornstarch and salt. Add water, egg yolks and lemon juice. Cook over medium heat, stirring constantly until slightly thickened. Remove form heat add lemon peel and butter and cool.

Use over gingerbread, cake squares, rice pudding, bread pudding, or serve plain in a dessert cup with a topping. This sauce has unlimited uses.

Mama's Gingerbread

1 cup brown sugar
½ cup shortening
2 eggs
¾ cup molasses
2 teaspoons baking soda
2 ¾ cups plain flour, sifted
2 teaspoons ginger
1 teaspoon cinnamon
½ teaspoon salt
1 cup buttermilk

Blend sugar, shortening and eggs. Stir in molasses. Add combined dry ingredients alternately with buttermilk and beat well. Pour in a well greased and floured 9 x 6 x 2-inch pan. Bake at 350° F for approximately 35 to 40 minutes. Serve warm. Best served either plain with butter, with a scoop of ice cream or with whipped cream.

I often put a glaze on this while hot.

Glaze

1 ½ cups powdered sugar
½ teaspoon vanilla flavoring
½ teaspoon butter, melted

Combine all ingredients. Add enough milk or cream to make it smooth.

Notes:

My maternal great-grandparents

Dr. Isaac Arnold and Susan Caroline "Meek" Herring

In memory of...
my maternal great-grandparents

Dr. Isaac Arnold and
Susan Caroline "Meek" Herring

Dr. Isaac Arnold Herring, D.D.S was born March 19, 1822 in Danville, Kentucky and died August 18, 1895.

Susan Caroline Meek Herring was born June 21, 1830 in York, South Carolina and died May 7, 1914. They are buried in Kosciusko City Cemetery in Kosciusko, Mississippi.

My great grandfather, Dr. Isaac Herring was originally from Danville, Kentucky and was the first licensed dentist to practice in Kosciusko, Mississippi. He was a member of the first graduating class at Ohio College of Dental Surgery in Cincinnati, Ohio in 1857. He also had part of a medical degree. He and his wife resided in Kosciusko at 603 South Natchez, which later burned. He acquired large tracts of land near Kosciusko to do his hunting and fishing. This is the land that now surrounds the Tracewood Community and into the swamp lands at Munson's Crossing. He was very active in community affairs. He was a founder of the First Presbyterian Church where he was an elder and led the congregational singing. This church building is now called The Mary Ricks Cultural Center. Great Grandfather Herring was a Captain in the Confederate States Army during the Civil War. My grandfather had a lot of great stories to tell of his father…remember this was in the horse and buggy days! My nephew has his dental tools today. Great Grandfather married Susan Caroline Meek August 16, 1853. She was the daughter of Abner and Eliza "Smith" Meek, descendants of Robert Meek, which came from Edinburgh, Scotland and finally settling in York County, South Carolina.

They had seven children:

Fannie Meek Herring, born January 19, 1855 and died December 10, 1880. She married Samuel H. McClintock January 22, 1880. Samuel H. McClintock was born October 9, 1847 in Belzoni, Mississippi and died November 24, 1923.

Carrie E. Herring, born January 25, 1858 and died February 10, 1930. On March 11, 1895 she married Samuel H. McClintock, her deceased sister's husband.

George Abner Herring was born January 23, 1861 and died December 16, 1934. He never married.

Mattie Virginia Herring was born December 14, 1861 and died April 5, 1918. She married George Mathew Noah September 30, 1884. George Noah was born December 14, 1861 and died April 5, 1918.

Annie Herring was born December 31, 1866 and died May 2, 1891.

Isaac Abner Herring, known as "Ike" was born February 17, 1869 and died December 26, 1955. He married Minnie Leola Herring February 8, 1903. She was born July 9, 1883 and died December 4, 1957.

Sue Herring was born August 5, 1871. She married H. F. Hammond December 15, 1898 and lived near Winona, Mississippi.

My great-grandparents had their hands full taking care of seven children with no modern conveniences. They had well water, oil lamps to read by and plenty of good homegrown food to eat. They treasured their horse back, horse and buggy or walking. These forms of transportation were the best they had so they enjoyed them greatly. My Grandfather spoke of prosperity in this family. I'm proud to be of their ancestry.

Crunchy Pecan Pie Crust 𝒦

1 cup plain flour
1 tablespoon sugar
1 stick margarine, softened
½ cup pecans, toasted and finely chopped

Combine all ingredients and mix until dough is formed. Press dough into a 10-inch pie plate. Prick sides and bottom of crust with a fork. Bake at 350° F for 15 minutes.

Use any type of custard or filling in this pie shell, chocolate, coconut, banana cream, etc.

Depression Pie Crust 1940

1 ¾ cups plain flour
¾ teaspoon salt
2/3 cup shortening
5 tablespoons ice water
2 9-inch pie pans

Preheat oven to 450° F

In a mixing bowl combine flour and salt. Mix well. Add shortening. Cut shortening into flour mixture with a pastry cutter or two dinner knives until the pieces are the size of peas. Sprinkle water, 1 tablespoon at a time over the mixture. With a fork work lightly together until all particles are moistened. Press dampened mixture into 2 balls. Do not handle any more than necessary. On a floured cloth or breadboard, sprinkle with flour. With a floured rolling pin roll dough 2 inches larger than the pie pan. Roll dough around rolling pin and lift to pie pan. Unroll and smooth dough to pan and prick the bottom and sides. Turn under top sides and flute with fingers. Bake for 15 minutes or until golden brown.

If possible chill crust in refrigerator before baking for 15 minutes. Can be used over cobblers. Freezes well.

Pie Crust ℋ

¾ cup shortening
½ teaspoon salt
2 cups plain flour
¼ cup cold water
2 9-inch pie pans

In a mixing bowl cut shortening in with flour and salt until the size of peas. Gradually add cold water by tablespoons until all is used. Press together to form 2 equal balls. On a floured cloth, place ball and press down using a floured rolling pin. Roll into a 12-inch circle. Lift gently into a 9-inch pie pan. Tuck under the sides and flute with fingers. Prick sides and bottom with a fork. If you do not have a rolling pin, try a fifth liquor bottle—I used one for years. Yields two 9-inch pie shells.

Magnificent Egg Custard Pie ℋ

4 eggs, beaten
1 ¼ cups sugar
½ stick butter, melted
1 teaspoon vanilla flavoring
2 cups milk
1 teaspoon flour
10-inch pie shell, unbaked and pricked

Mix all ingredients together, beating well. Pour into unbaked pie shell and bake on cookie sheet at 375° F for 10 minutes. Reduce heat to 200° F and continue baking until pie barely shakes.

If cooked on extremely high heat, pie filling will curdle and become watery.

Pie Shells—The All Occasion Pastry

Yields eight 9-inch pie shells

4 cups plain flour
1 tablespoons sugar
1 teaspoon baking powder
1 teaspoon salt
2 cups vegetable shortening
1 egg, beaten
1 teaspoon white vinegar
1 cup ice water

Combine all dry ingredients together and cut shortening in with a pastry cutter or two knives. Do this until it becomes the size of small peas. Place beaten egg with cold water and add to cut dry ingredients gradually until all of the water/egg mixture is used up. Roll into 8 balls. Chill for 2 hours. Roll out each ball with a floured rolling pin into a circle. (I use a floured cloth and keep the cloth stored in my refrigerator). Lay your pie pan over circle of dough and cut with a knife 1 ½ inches bigger than pie plate. Lift into pie tin or pan and turn under excess dough and flute with fingers. Always prick sides and bottom with a fork. This prevents crust from coming to the top. Repeat for all pie shells. Use immediately or wrap well and freeze until ready to use.

Pineapple Glaze Topping *K*

½ cup water
3 tablespoons cornstarch
¾ cup sugar
1 large can crushed pineapple, not drained
3 drops yellow food coloring

In a saucepan, combine all ingredients. Cook on medium heat until slightly thickened. Stir or blend well. Cool. Put a generous amount on pie that has been chilled.

This is also good on ice cream and between layers of cake.

1969 Chocolate Pie ᴷ (Rated a 10+)

3 tablespoons flour
1 ½ cups sugar
2 tablespoons cocoa
Pinch of salt
3 egg yolks
2 cups milk
½ stick butter
1 teaspoon vanilla flavoring
3 egg whites
1 teaspoon cream of tartar
½ cup sugar
1 teaspoon vanilla flavoring

Pie

In a mixing bowl, combine flour, sugar, cocoa, and salt. Make a well in center of mixture. Add egg yolks with a small amount of milk. With a hand mixer, blend mixture well. Add remaining milk and mix well. Pour into a heavy two-quart saucepan. Stir constantly on medium heat until mixture thickens. Remove from heat and add butter and vanilla. Beat for 30 seconds with a hand mixer until fluffy. Pour filling into a 9-inch pricked and pre-baked piecrust.

Meringue

In a glass or stainless mixing bowl, beat egg whites and cream of tartar at high speed until frothy (add sugar gradually). Add vanilla. Continue beating at high speed until mixture stands in peaks (should be stiff and glossy). Spread to edges of piecrust, completely sealing in filling. Bake until meringue is light brown.

You can double recipe to make filling for 3 pies. Can also substitute 1 cup flaky or grated coconut for cocoa to make coconut pie.

1940 Banana Cream Pie

9-inch deep dish pie shell, pricked and baked
2 tablespoons plain flour
1 tablespoon corn starch, heaping
¼ teaspoon salt
¾ cup sugar
3 egg yolks, beaten
2 cups milk
1 teaspoon vanilla flavoring
2 large bananas, sliced lengthwise ¼-inch thick

In a two-quart saucepan, combine flour, cornstarch, salt and sugar. Add egg yolks. Stir well. Add milk gradually while stirring until all is used. Cook over low heat stirring constantly until mixture thickens. Add vanilla. Cool. Place sliced bananas into bottom of pie shell. Cover with meringue.

Meringue

3 egg whites, room temperature
1/8 teaspoon salt
1 teaspoon vanilla flavoring
6 tablespoons sugar

In a 1 ½ quart mixing bowl combine egg whites and salt. Beat until peaks form. Add vanilla. Gradually add sugar until all is used. Spoon the meringue on the outer edges of the pie shell first and then fill in the center. Bake at 350° F for approximately 15 minutes or until golden brown.

Apple Pie

Two 10-inch unbaked pie shells, pricked
¾ cup sugar
1 ½ tablespoon plain flour
1 teaspoon cinnamon
Dash of nutmeg
Dash of salt
1 teaspoon vanilla flavoring
4 cups tart apples, thin-sliced
4 tablespoons butter, melted

In a large mixing bowl combine sugar, flour, spices, salt and vanilla. Mix well. Combine apples with mixture and toss until well coated. Place apple mixture into one 10-inch pricked, unbaked pie shells. Place dots of butter over apple filling. Cover top of apples with another 10-inch top crust and crimp edges together to seal. Cut 4 slits in top of pastry to allow steam to release. Place on cookie sheet in oven and bake at 350° F for approximately 35 to 40 minutes until crust is golden brown. Remove from oven and cool. Serve warm!

This requires two pie shells—one for the bottom and one for the top! Try brushing melted butter on the top of the piecrust and add a sprinkle of Vanilla-Cinnamon Sugar Sprinkle before baking. When serving, a scoop of ice cream or whipped cream makes this pie special!

Beatrice's Caramel Pie

¼ cup sugar, for caramelizing

Caramelized Sugar

Caramelize ¼ cup sugar by placing sugar into a skillet (preferably cast iron). Place skillet over low heat until sugar turns brown. Do not stir. Set aside.

1 ½ cups sugar
2 tablespoons flour
2 cups milk
3 egg yolks, beaten
1 stick butter
1 teaspoon vanilla flavoring

Pie

In a heavy saucepan, mix sugar, flour, milk and egg yolks. Cook over medium heat until mixture is thick. Add butter, vanilla and caramelized sugar. Beat until smooth with electric hand mixer. Pour into 9-inch pricked and pre-baked pie shell and cover with meringue. Bake at 350° F for 10 minutes or until meringue is light brown.

3 egg whites
1 teaspoon cream of tartar
6 teaspoons sugar
1 teaspoon vanilla flavoring

Meringue

In a glass or stainless mixing bowl, beat egg whites and cream of tartar at high speed until frothy (add sugar gradually). Add vanilla. Continue beating at high speed until mixture stands in peaks (should be stiff and glossy). Spread to edges of piecrust, completely sealing in filling. Bake until meringue is light brown.

Best-of-the-Best Chess Pie 10+

3 eggs, beaten
1 cup sugar
1 cup brown sugar
1 cup evaporated milk
½ stick butter, browned in skillet and cooled
1 tablespoon flour
1 teaspoon vanilla
1 tablespoon corn meal
10-inch unbaked pie shell, pricked

In a mixing bowl containing beaten eggs, add remaining ingredients. Beat 2 minutes and pour into unbaked pie shell. Bake at 300° F until barely shakes when tested. Cool. Serve lukewarm.

March 22, 1969 I gave birth to my son, Hugh Ronald Moore, in the Holmes County Community Hospital in Lexington, Mississippi. This pie was served the day I gave birth. I requested not to see my new born until I'd eaten due to my being so weak. This pie was so delicious that I requested another piece. I asked for the recipe and as you can see my wish was granted.

Strawberry Pie, A La Mode

10-inch deep dish pie shell, pricked, baked and cooled
1 ½ cups sugar
4 tablespoons corn starch
1 ¼ cups cold water
3-ounce box strawberry gelatin
2 pints fresh strawberries, washed, stemmed
Whipped cream or topping

In a saucepan, combine sugar and corn starch. Add water and stir. Cook on medium heat until slightly thickened. Remove from heat and pour in gelatin. Mix well until dissolved. Cool 20 minutes. Place strawberries into the empty pie shell. Spoon cooked and cooled mixture over strawberries and refrigerate for several hours before serving. Top with whipped cream just before serving. Yields 6 servings.

My dad's dog all dressed up
1920's

Buttermilk Chess Pie ᴷ

2 cups sugar
2 tablespoons flour
1 teaspoon corn meal
5 eggs, beaten
Zest of 1 lemon
2/3 cup buttermilk
1 stick butter, melted
1 teaspoon vanilla flavoring
9-inch pastry shell (unbaked with sides and bottom pricked with a fork)

Combine sugar, corn meal and flour in a mixing bowl; add beaten eggs, lemon zest and buttermilk. Stir until well mixed. Stir in butter and vanilla. Pour into unbaked pastry shell. Place on cookie sheet (makes crust brown and flaky) and bake at 350° F for 30 minutes or until pie barely shakes. Remove from oven and cool. Serve warm.

Zest is finely grated lemon rind! This pie freezes well. You can also add 1 cup flaked coconut and use a 10-inch pie shell instead of a 9-inch shell. Sometimes I top a piece of pie with a scoop of vanilla ice cream and microwave on medium for about 12 seconds. A la mode!

Late 1800's Candied Pecan Pie

1 tablespoon flour
1 cup sugar
3 eggs
1 ½ cups light corn syrup
3 or 4 cups pecans, toasted
1 teaspoon vanilla
10-inch deep-dish pie shell, unbaked and pricked

Mix flour and sugar. Add eggs. Mix well. Add light corn syrup, pecans and vanilla. Pour into unbaked piecrust. Bake at 225° F for 2 hours.

Double recipe to make three 9-inch standard pies! This is my grand-daughters' (Kristen and Karla) great-grandmother's recipe. Mrs. Gladys Davenport made these pies for years and sent several to her son – wherever he lived. They are thick and chewy!

Carrot Pie

3 eggs, beaten
¼ cup flour
1 ½ teaspoons baking powder
1 ½ cups sugar
½ teaspoon cinnamon
1 teaspoon vanilla flavoring
1 ½ pounds carrots (cooked, drained & mashed)
½ cup butter, melted
Powdered sugar (for sprinkling)
Unbaked 10-inch deep-dish pie shell

Combine eggs, flour, baking powder, sugar, cinnamon, vanilla, carrots and butter. Spoon into unbaked 10-inch pie shell or a large greased casserole dish. Bake at 350° F until mixture sets (does not shake). Cool. Sprinkle powdered sugar on top and serve warm.

Can substitute squash for carrots—very good!

Caramel Pie 𝒦

2 cups sugar (reserving ½ cup for caramelizing)
2 tablespoons flour
2 cups milk
4 egg yolks, beaten
3 tablespoons butter
1 teaspoon vanilla
9-inch pie shell, pricked and baked

Step 1: Caramelize sugar to make syrup: In a small iron skillet on low heat, slowly brown ½ cup of the sugar (will turn caramel looking).

Step 2: Mix remaining sugar, flour, milk, and egg yokes. Cook over hot water using a double boiler. Add caramel syrup to mixture. Cook until thick. Add butter and vanilla. Beat well. Pour into pie shell. Cool for 15 minutes in order for mixture to be used for a glaze on top. Add meringue on top of custard making sure the meringue covers all sides of the crust. Serve chilled. Delicious!

Meringue

3 egg whites
½ cup sugar
1 teaspoon vanilla flavoring

Beat 3 egg whites until stiff, gradually adding ½ cup sugar and 1 teaspoon vanilla. Spread over pie filling. Be sure to catch all sides of crust when spreading. Bake at 350° F until golden brown. Cool and serve.

Chess Pie 𝒦

6 eggs, beaten
2 cups sugar
1 teaspoon flour
1 teaspoon corn meal
Dash of salt
1 ½ cups milk (or half & half cream)
½ stick butter, melted
1 teaspoon vanilla flavoring
10-inch unbaked deep-dish pie shell

Combine eggs and sugar and beat. Add flour, corn meal, and salt and beat. Add milk, butter, and vanilla. Beat until well mixed. Pour into fluted & pricked pie shells. Bake on cookie sheets at 400° F for 10 minutes. Reduce to 275° F and bake until pie barely shakes. Remove from oven and allow pies to cool to room temperature before serving.

Baking uncooked piecrust with custard on a cookie sheet helps to brown bottom of piecrust. Can also bake in a cast iron skillet for even crunchier crust.

Coconut Cream Pie *K*

¾ cup sugar
3 tablespoons flour
1/8 teaspoon salt
2 cups milk
1 tablespoon butter, melted
3 egg yolks, beaten
2 teaspoons vanilla flavoring
1 cup shredded coconut
9-inch pie shell, pricked and baked

In a medium mixing bowl, combine sugar, flour and salt. Cream together for 1 minute. Add milk, butter, and beaten egg yolks. Cook on medium heat in a heavy saucepan until mixture thickens, but not stiff. Add vanilla and beat for 30 seconds with a hand beater, then fold in coconut. Pour into baked pie shell and set aside while preparing meringue. Note that this recipe can be doubled for three 9-inch pies.

Meringue

3 egg whites
½ cup sugar
1 teaspoon vanilla flavoring

Beat 3 egg whites until stiff, gradually adding ½ cup sugar and 1 teaspoon vanilla. Spread over pie filling. Be sure to catch sides of crust when spreading. Bake at 350° F until golden brown. Cool and serve.

I use this recipe for banana cream pie omitting coconut and adding sliced bananas to filling.

Devine No-Bake Pumpkin Pie

4 ounces cream cheese, softened
1 tablespoon milk (or half and half)
1 tablespoon sugar
1 ½ cups thawed whipped topping
1 graham cracker piecrust
1 cup milk (or half and half)
Two 4-ounce packages instant vanilla instant pudding
16-ounce can pumpkin
1 teaspoon cinnamon
½ teaspoon ginger
¼ teaspoon cloves

Step 1: Mix cream cheese, milk and sugar in large bowl with wire whisk until smooth. Gently fold in whipped topping. Spread onto bottom of crust.

Step 2: Pour 1 cup milk into bowl. Add pudding. Mix well, beat with wire whisk until well blended (1 to 2 minutes). Mixture will be thick.

Step 3: Stir in pumpkin and spices and mix well with wire whisk. Spread over cream cheese layer. Refrigerate at least 3 hours. Garnish with additional whipped topping and nuts if desired.

Yields 8 servings. I fold 1 teaspoon of vanilla into the whipped topping to enhance the flavor! Delicious!

Hawaiian Cream Cheese Pie – Simply Delicious ℋ

8 ounces cream cheese, softened
½ cup sugar
3 eggs, beaten
¼ cup lemon juice concentrate
1 14-ounce can condensed milk
10-inch deep-dish graham cracker crust

Combine cream cheese, sugar and eggs. Beat until well blended. Add lemon juice and condensed milk. Beat well. Pour into graham cracker crust. Bake at 300° F until barely shakes. Cool thoroughly. Add generous amount of Pineapple Glaze Topping. Refrigerate, and enjoy!

Pineapple Glaze Topping

½ cup water
3 tablespoons cornstarch
¾ cup sugar
1 large can crushed pineapple, not drained
3 drops yellow food coloring

In a saucepan, combine all ingredients. Cook on medium heat until slightly thickened. Stir or blend well. Cool. Put a generous amount on pie that has been chilled.

This is an all-occasion topping that is also good on ice cream and between layers of cake, etc. Other variations include strawberry, blueberry, or cherry for the topping instead of the pineapple.

P Nut Butter Cream Pie

8 ounces cream cheese, softened and beaten
1 cup sugar
1 cup creamy peanut butter
1 tablespoon butter
1 teaspoon vanilla flavoring
1 cup heavy cream (beaten stiff)
1 cup semi-sweet chocolate chips
3 tablespoons brewed coffee
Toasted peanuts for top coating (optional)
10-inch graham cracker crust pie shell

Beat cream cheese, sugar, peanut butter, butter and vanilla in a large bowl. Gently fold in half of beaten cream. Add and fold in remaining cream until all is invisible. Spread filling into pie shell and smooth the top.

Make the topping by combining the chocolate chips and coffee in a bowl. Cover and microwave on high for 1 ½ to 2 minutes. Stir until smooth. Allow to cool slightly and then pour over the top of smoothed filling. Refrigerate pie for 1 hour until chocolate is firm. Cover loosely and refrigerate overnight. Remove and sprinkle with toasted peanuts (if desired).

Yields 8 or more servings, depending on the size of your guest's sweet tooth. If desired, the pie may be topped with whipped cream topping instead of the chocolate chip and coffee topping or chocolate morsels. This is delicious either way.

Pappy Murdock's Pumpkin Pie

For two pies

6 eggs, beaten
1/3 cup evaporated milk (or half and half cream)
3 teaspoons flour, heaping
1½ cups sugar
½ cup dark corn syrup
2 tablespoons butter, melted
½ cup brown sugar
1 teaspoon cinnamon
2 cups unsweetened pumpkin, cooked
2 teaspoons vanilla flavoring
Two 9-inch unbaked pie shells, pricked

Mix all ingredients together well and pour mixture evenly into two
unbaked 9-inch pie shells (pricked). Bake at 350° F for approximately 40
minutes until the filling barely shakes. Remove pies from oven and allow
to cool.

*Best when served warm with whipped cream or vanilla ice cream topping.
Pie freezes well for serving at special occasions.*

Cherry Pie A La Mode *K*

2 14 ½-ounce cans tart cherries
6 tablespoons cornstarch
2 cups sugar
½ teaspoon salt
3 tablespoons butter
2 teaspoons vanilla flavoring
½ teaspoon almond flavoring
3-quart saucepan
2 9-inch pie shells, pricked and baked

Separate juice from cherries. In a saucepan, combine a small amount of cherry juice and cornstarch, mixing until dissolved. Add remaining juice, sugar, salt and butter. Mix well. Bring mixture to a boil, stirring constantly until thickened. Remove from heat! Add vanilla, almond and cherries. Divide filling evenly into two pre-baked pie shells. Cool and chill. Top with whipped cream or ice cream. Yields 6 servings per pie.

Old Fashioned Fried Fruit Pies ℐ

Use dried apples, peaches, or apricots for variety.

8 ounces dried apples
Water
3 teaspoons lemon juice
1 ½ cups sugar
½ stick butter
1 teaspoon cinnamon
2 teaspoons vanilla flavoring
10-count can of canned biscuits
Deep fat fryer with basket
Hot oil

In a 4-quart cooker place apples and cover with 4 inches of tap water above apples. Soak 4 hours or overnight. Drain water and add lemon juice and water 1 ½ inches below apples. Cook on medium heat until water is cooked out. Add sugar, butter, cinnamon and vanilla. Mix well, cool and refrigerate. Yields 5 cups of cooked apples.

On a generously floured cloth or dough board place one biscuit. With a floured rolling pin, roll biscuit into a 6-inch circle. Spoon 3 teaspoons of apple mixture on ½ of the circle of the biscuit smoothing with a spoon up to 1/8 inch of the edge of the circle of the biscuit. Bring other half of the circle over to the edge to meet and press edges lightly with index finger. Using a fork dipped in flour, press fork on 1/8 inch of edges of dough. Repeat until all is pressed with the fork. Gently turn filled dough over and repeat with fork. Make 3 pricks with the fork on top of pie. Immerse basket in oil to coat before placing filled biscuit into basket. (Prevents sticking). Place filled biscuit into basket and fry until golden brown. Remove and place on paper towel. Repeat process. Serve warm. Yields 10 fried pies.

There will be apple mixture left over. This is called apple butter...great on toast, biscuit, between cake layers, etc. In the 1800s, cooks used home-made biscuit dough to make these pies. I usually shortcut the procedure by using canned biscuits.

Poor Man's Oatmeal Pie

9-inch unbaked picked pie shell
2 eggs, beaten
1 cup sugar
1 cup dark corn syrup
1 cup quick rolled oats
1 teaspoon vanilla flavoring
½ cup melted butter

Preheat oven to 350° F. In a mixing bowl combine eggs and sugar and heat well. Add corn syrup, oats, vanilla and butter and mix well. Pour into pie shell and bake for 20 minutes or until barely shakes. Serve warm. Yields 6 servings.

Heavenly Pecan Pie *K*

4 eggs, beaten
¾ cup brown corn syrup
1 cup dark brown sugar (packed)
1 teaspoon vanilla flavoring
1 stick butter, browned in skillet and cooled
1 cup pecans, chopped
1 cup pecans, halves

Combine eggs, corn syrup, brown sugar and vanilla and beat 30 seconds. Scorch or brown butter in a skillet (do not burn). Cool a little. Add browned butter to mixture. Mix well. Spread chopped nuts into a 10-inch unbaked pie shell (pricked with a fork). Pour mixture over pecans. Place pecan halves over the entire pie filling and dunk them once. Place pie on a cookie sheet in 350° F oven and bake until the pie barely shakes. Remove from the oven and cool. Serve with scoop of ice cream or whipped cream.

My mother always believed in toasting the pecans and browning the butter to enhance the taste in many of her delicious dishes.

Raisin-Walnut Pie

1 cup white corn syrup
3 large eggs, beaten
½ cup sugar
½ stick butter, softened
½ teaspoon grated lemon rind
¼ teaspoon salt
1 teaspoon allspice
1 cup raisins, soak in warm water for 5 minutes, then drained
1 cup chopped walnuts, toasted and cooled

In a medium mixing bowl, combine corn syrup, eggs, sugar, butter, lemon rind, salt and allspice. Mix well! Add raisins and nuts. Pour into 9-inch unbaked pricked pie shell. Bake in preheated 400° F oven for 10 minutes. Reduce heat to 350° F and bake 30 to 35 minutes longer. Remove from oven and serve warm with a scoop of vanilla ice cream (optional).

Preheat oven – place pricked pie shell into skillet and pour mixture in. This guarantees a crunchy brown bottom piecrust.

Lemon Ice Box Pie

3 egg yolks, beaten
14-ounce can condensed milk
½ cup lemon juice
1 teaspoon grated lemon rind
2 drops yellow food coloring
3 egg whites
1 teaspoon cream of tartar (optional)
¼ cup sugar (4 tablespoons)
1 teaspoon vanilla flavoring
9-inch graham cracker pie shell

Pie

Preheat oven to 350° F. In medium bowl, beat egg yolks and combine with milk, lemon juice, lemon rind and food coloring. Beat well. Pour filling into a prepared 9-inch graham cracker pie shell. Place meringue on top of pie and bake at 350° F until light brown. May top pie with whipped cream or cool whip instead of meringue.

Meringue

In a glass or stainless mixing bowl, beat egg whites and cream of tartar at high speed until frothy. Add sugar gradually. Add vanilla and fold. Continue beating at high speed until mixture stands in peaks (should be stiff and glossy). Spread meringue to edges of shell, completely sealing in filling. Bake until meringue is light brown. Cool and chill before serving. Yields 6 servings.

Southern Pecan Pie

3 eggs, slightly beaten
1 cup white sugar
½ cup brown sugar
3 tablespoons butter, melted
3 tablespoons corn meal
1 cup dark corn syrup
Dash of salt
1 teaspoon vanilla flavoring
1 cup pecans, chopped and toasted in oven for 15 minutes at 200° F
9-inch unbaked pie shell, pricked

Beat eggs and sugars. Add butter and corn meal. Beat hard for 3 minutes. Add corn syrup, salt, vanilla, and cooled pecans and salt. Beat 3 minutes longer. Pour in unbaked pie shell. Bake at 350° F for 15 minutes on cookie sheet or cast iron skillet for flaky, brown crust. Reduce oven to 200° F and bake about 30 minutes. Cool. Serve warm. Yields 6 servings.

The more you beat this the better!

Sweet Potato Chess Pie ᴷ

For 3 pies:	For 12 pies:
4 or 5 eggs	16 to 20
3 cups sugar	12 cups
6 tablespoons flour, heaping	24 tablespoons
½ teaspoon salt	2 teaspoons
3 tablespoons corn meal	12 tablespoons
2 cups sweet potatoes, cooked, drained and mashed	8 cups
2 sticks butter, melted	8 sticks
1 cup evaporated milk	4 cups
2 teaspoons vanilla flavoring	8 teaspoons
2 teaspoons ground cinnamon	8 teaspoons
3 9-inch unbaked pie shells, pricked	12 shells

Beat eggs. Add sugar, flour, salt and corn meal and beat well. Add potatoes, butter, milk, flavoring and cinnamon and beat 1 minute. Distribute evenly into three unbaked & pricked 9-inch pie shells. Bake at 350° F until pies barely shake.

This is my personal physician Dr. John G. Downer's favorite pie. I usually make 12 pies when I bake. A single pie lasts only one meal in my house. They're great when served warm with vanilla ice cream or whipped cream. Homegrown sweet potatoes work the best — especially the Puerto Rico variety. The pies freeze well and are great when unexpected occasions or personal cravings pop up.

Lemon Meringue Pie $^{\mathcal{K}}$

1 ½ cups sugar
4 tablespoons cornstarch
Dash of salt
1 ¼ cups cold water
2 large egg yolks, beaten well
6 tablespoons fresh lemon juice
2 tablespoons butter
2 teaspoons finely grated lemon peel
9-inch baked pie shell

In a heavy saucepan mix sugar, cornstarch and salt. Add water, beaten egg yolks, and lemon juice. Cook over medium heat until mixture thickens, stirring constantly. Remove from heat. Add butter and lemon peel and mix. Pour into baked pie shells. Add meringue and brown at 350° F.

Can be used as a sauce for bread pudding or as a filling for split-layer cakes.

Meringue

3 egg whites
¼ cup sugar
1 teaspoon vanilla flavoring

Beat 3 egg whites until stiff, gradually adding sugar and vanilla. Spread over pie filling. Be sure to catch sides of crust when spreading. Bake at 350° F until golden brown. Cool and serve.

Walnut Pie 𝒦

3 eggs, slightly beaten
1 cup light brown sugar, firmly packed
¼ cup butter (scorched light brown in skillet and cooled)
1 teaspoon vanilla flavoring
1 cup walnuts, chopped and toasted
9-inch unbaked pie shell

In a mixing bowl, add eggs, sugar, cooled butter and vanilla flavoring. Beat 2 minutes. Stir in walnuts and pour into unbaked pie shell. Bake at 350° F for 35 minutes or until pie barely shakes. Cool before cutting. I serve this pie at room temperature or slightly warmed.

I've made this using 1 cup flaked coconut (use a 10-inch crust) – optional – it's delicious either way!

Banana Pudding 𝒦

3 eggs, beaten
1 cup sugar
3 tablespoons flour
Dash of salt
4 cups milk
1 ½ teaspoons vanilla flavoring
6 bananas
1 large package vanilla wafers

Combine eggs, sugar, flour and salt and beat well. Pour mixture into milk. Cook until slightly thickened. Add vanilla and stir. Allow mixture to cool. Pour over layer of bananas and vanilla wafers and chill.

This is very good.

No Bake Banana Pudding

8 ounces sour cream
3 ½-ounce package instant vanilla pudding
3 ½ cups milk
3 bananas
1 package vanilla wafers
8 ounces whipped topping
1 teaspoon vanilla flavoring

Mix sour cream, vanilla pudding, and milk until thickened. Layer with vanilla wafers and bananas in large container. Fold vanilla flavoring into whipped topping and spoon onto pudding. Chill. This will keep for days refrigerated.

Instant Banana Pudding

14-ounce can condensed sweetened milk
1 ½ cups cold water
3 ½-ounce package instant vanilla pudding
2 cups whipping cream, whipped
36 vanilla wafers
4 medium bananas, sliced

In a large mixing bowl combine condensed milk and water. Add pudding mix and beat well. Chill approximately six minutes. Fold in whipped cream. In a large serving dish, layer pudding, banana slices, and wafers. Repeat. Top with vanilla wafers. Spread pudding last covering all. Chill. Yields 12 servings.

Sliced bananas will not turn brown as fast when lemon juice is sprinkled on them prior to using.

Rice Pudding *K*

5 eggs
1 ¼ cups sugar
2 tablespoons flour
1 teaspoon corn meal
¼ teaspoon cinnamon
Dash of salt
3 cups milk
1 stick butter, melted
2 ½ cups rice, cooked and cool
1 teaspoon vanilla flavoring
1 cup raisins
3 slices brown bread (optional)
Dash of cinnamon for sprinkling

Beat eggs. Add sugar and beat well. Add flour, corn meal, cinnamon, and salt. Stir well. Add milk and butter and stir. Add cooked rice, vanilla and raisins and stir. Pour mixture into greased casserole container. Tear brown bread apart and arrange on top of custard. Dunk bread into mixture until well saturated. Sprinkle a little cinnamon or nutmeg on top. Bake in slow oven at 300° F until barely shakes. Remove from oven. Serve warm. Use whipped cream or ice cream for a topping if desired.

My husband Dutch's eyes light up when he smells this cooking or sees the cooked dish on the stove.

Rice & Biscuit Pudding ᴷ

Use a 2-quart, buttered casserole dish.
4 eggs
1 cup sugar, heaped
2 teaspoons flour
1 teaspoon corn meal
2 teaspoons vanilla flavoring
2 ½ cups milk
2 cups rice, cooked and cooled
1 stick butter, melted (reserve ½ of melted butter for topping)
3 biscuits, (cooked and split into halves)
Sprinkle with ½ cup chopped walnuts or pecans
Nutmeg or cinnamon on top

Beat eggs, sugar, flour, corn meal and vanilla until well mixed. Add milk, rice and ½ of melted butter. Mix well. Place split biscuits onto bottom of casserole dish with cut sides face down. Pour mixture over biscuit. Let stand for about 15 minutes in order for biscuits to soak up liquid mixture. Dunk several times if needed. Last of all sprinkle chopped nuts over mixture then add cinnamon or nutmeg (I prefer cinnamon). Pour remaining butter over the mixture. Bake at 300° F until the custard sets or barely shakes. Brown slightly (using broiler). Remove and cool. Serve warm.

Optional! Can use ½ cup coconut, ½ cup of raisins. You can also use torn apart brown bread slices in place of the biscuits. Biscuit pudding was made in the olden days for desert due to having fresh eggs, butter and cream from cow's milk. This dessert was even called "Poor Man's Dessert" but is so tasty it is fit for a king!

Butter Roll ᴷ

2 teaspoons vanilla flavoring
½ cup sugar
½ cup butter, melted
2 cups biscuit dough (use "Mama's Biscuits" recipe)
Enough milk to cover

Mix vanilla, sugar and melted butter together in order to make a mixture.

Make up biscuit dough. Lift out on floured cloth or board. With rolling pin, roll to 1/8-inch thickness into a square. Brush vanilla, sugar, and butter mixture generously all over square. Roll up square like a jellyroll. Cut into ½-inch pieces and stand in 9-inch square butter greased baking dish. Cover with milk and bake at 350° F for approximately 30 minutes or until slightly brown. Serve warm.

Optional—Before baking, sprinkle with cinnamon, toasted chopped nuts, additional ½ cup brown sugar, ¼ cup melted butter and 1 cup raisins. This is the version I prefer! Yields 6 servings.

Dr. Isaac A. Herring, D.D.S.

Cobbler ℋ

½ cup butter
1 cup sugar
1/8 teaspoon salt
1 teaspoon vanilla flavoring
1 cup plain flour
2/3 cup milk
2 teaspoons baking powder
3 cups of your favorite fruit
9-inch square baking dish

Melt butter in large baking dish. Mix all ingredients together except fruit until smooth and pour over melted butter in dish. After pouring into butter DO NOT STIR OR DISTURB! Add fruit and juice of your choice. Again DO NOT STIR OR DISTURB! Bake at 350° F for approximately 35 minutes or until brown. Yields 5 to 8 servings.

This recipe works well for sweetened peaches, blackberries, cherries, pears, and apples, etc.

Walnut Cinnamon Rolls *K*

1 cup boiling water
¾ cup sugar
1 cup shortening
2 eggs, beaten
2 packages yeast
1 cup warm water
5 ½ cups sifted plain flour
1 teaspoon salt
1 teaspoon vanilla
2 cups walnuts, chopped
2 cups raisins
2 sticks butter, melted
1 teaspoon cinnamon

Pour boiling water over the first three ingredients. Cool! Add eggs, then yeast (which has been dissolved in warm water). In a large bowl, combine flour and salt. Pour mixture over the flour. Beat until elastic like. Cover with a white cloth and put in a warm place allowing the mixture to rise until double its size in bulk. Press the mixture down. On a large generously floured dough cloth or board, roll dough into a complete square 1/8-inch thick. Mix vanilla, walnuts, raisins, butter and cinnamon together and spread evenly over the dough. Gently roll up dough and seal the edges. Cut dough into 1-inch thick cross-wise sections (rolls). Place rolls flat into three 13 x 9 x 2-inch, greased baking pans—allowing 2 inches between each and set aside to rise for 20 minutes. Bake at 350° F until golden brown or approximately 20 minutes. Remove from oven and cool 10 minutes. Glaze. Yields 40 rolls.

Glaze

1 pound powdered sugar
3 teaspoons butter, melted
1 teaspoon vanilla flavoring
Milk

Combine all ingredients in a medium bowl. Add just enough milk to ensure spreading consistency. Spoon over hot rolls and enjoy!

The cinnamon roll recipe is great for making glazed donuts. Omit the ingredients that aren't normally found in doughnuts—walnuts, butter, cinnamon and raisins. Cut with donut cutter and deep fry on medium high heat. Remove from oil. Place on paper towel. Then spread with glaze and place onto waxed paper or wire rack to cool.

Whipped Cream ℋ

1 cup whipping cream
2 tablespoons powdered sugar
Hand mixer, chilled bowl and beaters

In a mixing bowl, beat cream until cream starts to thicken. Add sugar while beating. When peaks form, quit beating. Add flavoring and fold. Yields 2 cups.

This is great on custard pies without meringue, fruit pies, as a topping for hot chocolate, strawberry short cake, folding into fruit salads. My daddy would say, "whipped cream makes anything taste good!"

Notes:

Notes:

Notes:

My maternal great-grandparents

*Great-grandfather John Russel "Poss" Herring and his daughter
(my grandmother) Minnie Leola "Herring" Herring.
Photo unavailable of his wife Bell "Farris" Herring.*

In memory of...
my maternal great-grandparents

John Russell and Bell "Farris" Herring.

John Russell Herring was born December 13, 1861 and died April 11, 1953. Bell "Farris" Herring was born in September 1861 and died in November 1899. They are buried in Kosciusko City Cemetery.

John Russell "Poss" Herring was the son of John "Frosty" and Rosanna "Pittman" Herring. He married Bell Farris. They had six children. My great grandmother Bell died in 1899 when my grandmother Minnie was sixteen years old. Their children were:

Minnie Leola "Herring" Herring, settled in Kosciusko, Mississippi.

Della "Herring" Buntyn, settled in Laurel, Mississippi.

Clyde "Herring" Halliday, settled in Laurel, Mississippi.

Georgia "Herring" Thornton, settled in Morton, Mississippi.

Breland Herring, information unavailable

Luther Herring, settled in Bovina, east of Vicksburg, Mississippi.

John Russell "Poss" Herring married his second wife Zula Ophelia Therrell November 7, 1900. They had two daughters:

Johnnie Ruth Herring. She never married. She lived in Kosciusko and Jackson Mississippi and later settled in New Orleans, Louisiana. Before her death she moved to Gulfport, Mississippi.

Julia "Herring" Crozier made her home in Memphis, Tennessee then later moved to New Orleans, Louisiana where she lived for many years. She is buried in Memphis, Tennessee.

Granddad, as we called him, then married Mollie Claitor. When Mollie died, Granddad married his fourth wife, who we called Miss Estelle. She outlived my grandfather and he lived to be 92 years old. Granddad had strong beliefs about certain issues — no one could change his mind — might say he was a bit stubborn about his principles!

Granddad was the fourth of twelve children. He lived most of his younger years in rural Carroll County near Vaiden, Mississippi and raised his family there. He later moved to Kosciusko, Mississippi. His residence and farm were located on South Huntington Street, across from Parkway Cemetery. He worked for the railroad. I remember he would pull out his railroad watch to check the time of day. He had a large garden every year and stocked his pantry with jars of vegetables for the winter. He had an orchard of fruit trees. He canned and dried the fruit for making delicious fruit pies. His front yard was full of pecan trees, which he climbed and pruned until he was ninety years old. Honey with the comb was served at every meal.

Granddad would say grace before every meal starting on an extremely high pitch, then graduating to words that we could not hear and then say a resounding "Amen." We always got tickled when he said grace. My mother said that Granddad saved ninety cents of every dollar that he made.

Granddad had a big white, wood-framed home with a porch that went nearly all the way around. The porch had a swing on each end with padding on the seat and a pillow at the back in order to lie down and rest your head.

We would ride with Granddad on occasions — always sitting in the back seat. I don't believe he ever really knew how to drive a straight stick or manual transmission because we were getting the jolt of our lives when he would take off. In fact, the car would jerk for the first block. Then, he would shift to second gear and we jerked a while longer. I don't recall him ever taking the car out of second gear. When we finally reached town, he would usually buy us an ice cream cone. We would always look forward to his starting the car again. We felt as though we'd been on a roller coaster when we returned to his home.

Granddad always gave several dollars when a person graduated from high school and several more when one finished college to total five dollars, which was nice of him but a little strange. He was one of the fortunate ones to have a refrigerator. It was kept on high so that the water was just under freezing when he wanted water to drink. He had a hearing problem and had to wear a hearing aid.

I didn't know my great grandmother. I did know my great grandfather's sister, Aunt Arvie "Herring" Montague of Vaiden. We occasionally visited her. She had a large home in the country on a hill. One bedroom was separated from the rest of the home. I don't know who slept in the "remote" room. Her son Tom and family lived in the valley. Tom had a daughter my age named Lucile.

I enjoyed knowing my great granddad. He was a hard worker and lived comfortably until he died. His children visited him regularly.

Chocolate Chip Cookies 𝒦

2 eggs, beaten
1 cup butter
¾ cup sugar
¾ cup light brown sugar
1 teaspoon vanilla flavoring
2 ½ cups flour, plain
1 teaspoon soda
1 teaspoon salt
1 cup chopped walnuts (or pecans)
12 ounces semi-sweet chocolate morsels

Combine flour, soda and salt; set aside. In a large mixing bowl combine the first 5 ingredients and blend well. Stir in nuts. Add flour mixture and mix well. Drop by teaspoonfuls onto greased cookie sheets. Bake at 350° F for 8 to 11 minutes or until edges are brown. Remove from oven with pancake turner onto a brown grocery bag. Cool completely. Store in an airtight container. Makes approximately 5 dozen.

I sometimes substitute butterscotch morsels for the chocolate morsels or you can mix the two. They are delicious either way. Cookies should be moist and chewy.

Cinnamon Sugar 𝒦

2 tablespoons cinnamon
1 cup sugar

Mix together and store in a sealed jar or saltshaker. Yields approximately 1 cup.

A big spice shaker is the perfect container for this! For butter toast, pies, pie crust topping, puddings, ice cream, cookie topping, French toast, etc.

Easy World War II Oatmeal Cookies 𝒦

¾ cup lard or shortening, softened
½ cup sugar, plus 1 tablespoon
1 cup brown sugar, packed
1 egg, beaten
¼ cup buttermilk
1 teaspoon vanilla flavoring
1 cup plain flour
3 cups rolled oats, uncooked
¾ teaspoon salt
½ teaspoon soda
1 teaspoon cinnamon
2 cups pecans or walnuts, chopped

In a large mixing bowl cream lard or shortening, sugars, and egg until blended well. Add buttermilk and flavoring and mix well. Mix all dry ingredients together. Add to mixture and mix well. Drop by teaspoonful onto well-greased cookie sheets and bake at 350° F for approximately 12 to 15 minutes. Yields six-dozen cookies.

I do not use lard today; use vegetable shortening! My mother and I made these oatmeal cookies from 1948 to 1953 and sent them to my brother who was in the U.S. Armed Services. He said everyone would gather around when he got a box of goodies from home. Mother and I sent these on a regular basis.

Shortbread Sugar Cookies

¾ cup vegetable shortening (or butter)
1 cup sugar
2 eggs, beaten
1 teaspoon vanilla flavoring
½ teaspoon lemon flavoring
2 ½ cups self-rising flour
Sugar

Step 1: In a medium-sized mixing bowl, cream shortening and sugar until fluffy. Add in eggs and flavorings and mix well. Add flour. Stir well until blended and chill.

Step 2: After chilled, roll dough thin with floured rolling pin on a floured board or cloth. Cut with 3-inch cookie cutter. Sprinkle with sugar before baking. Bake at 400° F for 6 to 8 minutes on ungreased baking sheet until edges of cookies are lightly browned. Remove from cookie sheet onto brown grocery sack or cookie rack and allow to cool.

For fruit-filled cookies, put 2 uncooked cut cookie dough patties together with 1 teaspoon fruit filling in the center. Seal—press edges together with your index finger. Sprinkle with sugar and bake. Yields two-dozen filled cookies. Suggestions for filling are: strawberry, peach, or apricot preserves, plum jelly or blackberry jam —your choice.

Old Fashioned Depression Tea Cakes *K*

1 ¾ cups sugar
1 cup shortening or lard
2 eggs, beaten
3 cups plain flour
½ teaspoon soda
½ teaspoon salt
1 teaspoon cinnamon
1 teaspoon vanilla or lemon flavoring

In a large mixing bowl, cream together sugar and shortening. Add eggs and beat until well mixed. Work in remaining ingredients and chill. Roll into 4 balls.

Taking 1 ball out of refrigerator and roll 1/8-inch thick on a floured board or cloth with a rolling pin. Cut dough with a 2 ½-inch cookie cutter. Place onto greased cookie sheets. Bake at 350° F for 7 to 10 minutes or until crusty and light brown around the edges. Remove with a pancake turner. Place onto a brown grocery sack until cooled thoroughly. Repeat process. Store in an airtight container until ready to serve. Cookies should be soft and slightly chewy.

Great with milk or coffee! Most people of the 1930s did not put cinnamon in their teacakes. This dough recipe can be used to cut all kinds of shapes with cookie cutters.

Molasses Tea Cakes

1 ½ cups sugar
1 cup lard or shortening
2 eggs, beaten
1 cup dark molasses
4 cups flour
4 teaspoons soda
2 teaspoons cinnamon
1 teaspoon ginger
1 teaspoon salt
1 teaspoon vanilla flavoring

In a large mixing bowl, cream together sugar and shortening. Add eggs and molasses. Beat until well blended. Knead together remaining ingredients.

On a floured board or cloth work up ¼ of mixture at a time. Roll or pat out until dough is 1/8-inch thick. Cut dough with a floured 2 ½-inch diameter cookie cutter. Place on greased cookie sheets and bake at 350° F for 8 to 10 minutes until crust is crusty looking. Remove from pans and place on a brown grocery bag to cool. Store in an airtight container until ready to use. Yields approximately 5 dozen cookies.

Cookies, candies, cakes, brownies, and breads make excellent all occasion gifts.

Frosted Orange Tea Cakes *K* 10+

1 ¾ cups sugar
1 stick butter, softened
1 stick margarine, softened
2 teaspoons orange flavoring
2 eggs, beaten
3 cups all-purpose flour
½ teaspoon soda
¼ teaspoon salt
Flour for kneading

Sift all dry ingredients and set aside. In a large mixing bowl, cream together sugar, butter, margarine and flavoring. Add eggs—stirring until well mixed. Add dry ingredients slowly to mixture, mixing well. Turn out mixture onto a floured cloth or board—dividing evenly into three long rolls. Place rolls onto floured waxed paper, rolling up and chilling until firm (1 to 4 hours).

To bake, slice 1/8-inch thick and place onto lightly greased cookie sheets. Bake at 325° F for 8 to 10 minutes. Remove from oven and transfer cookies to cookie rack or brown paper bag to cool. Yields 4 dozen cookies. Great for rolling and cutting into shapes.

To make plain tea cakes, omit orange flavoring and add 2 teaspoons vanilla and ½ teaspoon cinnamon.

Cream Cheese Frosting

8 ounces cream cheese, room temperature
½ stick butter or margarine
1 pound powdered sugar
1 teaspoon orange flavoring
2 drops food coloring
1 cup walnuts, chopped

In a medium mixing bowl, cream together cream cheese, butter, flavoring and food coloring. Gradually add sugar. Add nuts—stirring until well mixed. Frost each tea cake. Allow enough time for the frosting to dry out on top before serving.

Real Old Fashion Tea Cakes

2 eggs, beaten
2 cups sugar
2/3 cups milk
2/3 cups butter (or lard), room temperature
2 teaspoons vanilla flavoring
1 teaspoon lemon flavoring (optional)
Flour, self-rising

Mix all ingredients together and blend well. Add enough self-rising flour to make a stiff dough. Roll out on floured cloth and cut with a 2 ½-inch cutter. Place onto greased cookie sheet and bake in preheated oven. Bake at 350° F until edges of cookies are golden brown (about 10 minutes). Remove from sheet and place onto brown paper. Cool.

This recipe came from an old book I found while cleaning the family home.

Apple Butter *K*

Use dried apples, peaches, or apricots for variety.

8 ounces dried apples
Water
3 teaspoons lemon juice
1 ½ cups sugar
½ stick butter
1 teaspoon cinnamon
2 teaspoons vanilla flavoring

In a 4-quart cooker place apples and cover with 4 inches of tap water above apples. Soak 4 hours or overnight. Drain water and add lemon juice and water 1 ½ inches below apples. Cook on medium heat until tender. Add sugar, butter, cinnamon and vanilla. Mash with a potato masher. Mix well, cool and refrigerate. Yields 5 cups of cooked apple butter.

This is usually served on biscuit, toast or as a side dish.

Chewy Coconut Cookies

1 ½ cups moist canned coconut
½ cups sugar
3 tablespoons flour
1/8 teaspoons salt
2 egg whites
½ teaspoon vanilla flavoring
½ teaspoon almond flavoring

In a medium mixing bowl, combine coconut, sugar, flour and salt. Stir in egg whites and flavorings and mix well. Drop by teaspoon on greased cookie sheet. Bake at 325° F for 20 minutes or until edges of cookies are golden brown. Remove and cool on both sides then store in dry container. Yields 2 dozen cookies.

Mountain Molasses Taffy Candy

2/3 cup molasses
1 ½ teaspoons white vinegar
1 teaspoon vanilla
2 cups white sugar
2/3 cup boiling water
¼ teaspoon baking soda
2 tablespoons butter

In a 3-quart heavy saucepan, mix all of the ingredients except the baking soda and butter. Cook until brittle or a hard ball forms when a small amount is dropped into cold water. Remove from heat. Immediately add soda and stir well. Pour onto a buttered 10-inch platter. When cool enough to handle, grease your hands with butter. Pull a little taffy at a time. When taffy is light, pull into a long rope and cut with scissors. Wrap individually in wax paper and twist the ends in opposite directions. Store in airtight containers.

For many years when cars were not available people would have taffy pulling parties...quite a big "to do" in the olden times especially for the young people. This was one way of extending community good will as well as fellowship.

Eloise's Fruit Cake Cookies

1 cup brown sugar
½ stick butter, softened
4 eggs, well beaten
1 teaspoon baking soda
½ teaspoon nutmeg
1 small glass whiskey (4 to 6 ounces)
1 teaspoon vanilla flavoring
3 tablespoons milk
3 cups plain flour
1 pound raisins
1 pound candied pineapple, chopped
1 pound candied cherries, chopped
1 ½ pounds chopped pecans, chopped
Greased cookie sheets
Preheat oven to 350° F

Mix soda with flour and sift. Beat sugar, butter, eggs, nutmeg, whiskey,
vanilla, and milk and mix until well blended. Add 1 ½ cups flour mixture
and mix. Take remaining 1 ½ cups of flour and mix with chopped fruit and
pecans. Add fruits, nuts and flour to mixture and mix well. Drop by
tablespoonfuls on greased cookie sheet. Bake 15 minutes. Remove from
pan onto brown paper or wire rack. Cool and store in airtight container.
Yields a lot of cookies.

Fantasy Fudge

3 cups sugar
¾ cup butter
2/3 cup evaporated milk
7-ounce jar marshmallow crème
12 ounces chocolate chips
1 cup chopped walnuts (or pecans)

Combine sugar, butter, and milk. Bring to a full rolling boil stirring constantly. Continue stirring until thermometer reaches 234° F. Add marshmallow crème, chocolate chips and nuts. Mix well. Pour into a greased 13 x 9-inch pan. Cool and cut into desired sizes or 2 x 2-inch size. Yields about 24 squares.

Chocolate Fudge ᴷ

3 cups sugar
¾ cup cocoa
Dash of salt
1 ½ cups milk or half & half cream
½ stick butter
2 teaspoons vanilla flavoring
1 cup nuts, chopped

Step 1: Combine sugar, cocoa and salt. Add milk and mix well.

Step 2: In a large heavy saucepan put Step 1 ingredients. Cook on high heat until this mixture comes to a rolling boil. Reduce heat and boil until a hard ball forms when dropped into cold water. Remove from heat and add butter and vanilla flavoring. Mix well. Add nuts and beat until thickened. Will thicken more as the mixture cools. Pour into greased 12 x 8-inch platter, cool and cut into small squares. When completely cold on both sides, store in airtight container.

I have made this since I was very young. Good! I use this for frosting on my 3-layer stack cake. Delicious.

Chocolate Fudge

2 sticks butter
1 pint marshmallow cream
3 6-ounce packages chocolate chips
3 cups chopped pecans
2 teaspoons vanilla flavoring
4 ½ cups sugar
12-ounce can evaporated milk
11 x 7 x 2-inch oblong pan greased with butter

In a mixing bowl, cut up butter and add all ingredients except sugar and milk. Set aside. Mix sugar and milk in a skillet or heavy saucepan. Bring to a boil and boil for 9 minutes, stirring constantly to keep from sticking. Pour over other ingredients in bowl and mix well. Pour into oblong pan. Refrigerate several hours before cutting into squares. Yields 4 pounds of candy.

"Cut Out" Cookie Dough

1 stick butter
2/3 cup brown sugar
1/3 cup white sugar
1 teaspoon vanilla flavoring
1 egg, beaten
1 ½ cups plain flour
¼ teaspoon cream of tartar
¼ teaspoon salt
½ teaspoon cinnamon

Cream butter, sugars and vanilla and add beaten egg. Combine dry ingredients and add to creamed mixture and mix well. Chill until ready to bake.

To bake: Pat out onto floured cloth or wax paper. Cut into any shape you desire. Bake at 375° F for 2 to 8 minutes.

To avoid using more flour, you can sprinkle powdered sugar onto wax paper to prevent cookie dough from sticking.

Meringue Shells K

For ice cream, fill meringues with ice cream and drizzle with chocolate sauce.

3 egg whites (room temperature)
Dash of salt
¼ teaspoon cream of tartar
1 teaspoon vanilla flavoring
1 cup sugar

In a glass or stainless mixing bowl, beat egg whites, salt and cream of tartar. Add vanilla. Beat whites at high speed until frothy. Gradually add sugar (a little at a time). Continue beating at high speed until mixture stands in peaks (should be stiff and glossy). Line a cookie sheet with aluminum foil. Spoon out heaping tablespoonful mounds onto foil, leaving room for mounds to expand. Bake 1 hour at 275° F. Turn off heat and leave cookie sheet in the oven until cool. Remove from oven. Gently remove meringue shells from the foil.

These are crunchy. They're good by themselves, but better when filled with ice cream.

Butter Toffee Candy

1 cup sugar
½ teaspoon salt
¼ cup water
½ cup butter
12 ounces chocolate chips, melted
2 cups walnuts or pecans, chopped

In a medium saucepan mix well first three ingredients. Add butter and cook on stove until butter melts. <u>Do not stir any more</u>! Using candy thermometer, boil mixture until it reaches 285° F or until hard ball forms when dropped in cold water. Pour into buttered pan and cool in refrigerator. When mixture has cooled, spread with half of the melted chocolate. Sprinkle with half of the chopped nuts. Cool and turn out onto wax paper and spread with remaining chocolate and nuts. Cool and break into pieces. Store in an airtight container in the refrigerator. Serve as needed. Yields 2 pounds of candy.

Two Step Peanut Butter Balls 𝒦

½ cup butter
1 pound jar peanut butter, creamy
1 teaspoon vanilla flavoring
1 ½ pounds powered sugar
Milk chocolate morsels (12-ounce size, melted over boiling water)
1 tablespoon paraffin wax

Step 1: Knead first four ingredients together and form into balls the size of walnuts. Let dry out for 1 hour.

Step 2: Melt and stir chocolate morsels and wax over hot water inserting a toothpick in the top of a ball and dip or dunk into the chocolate mixture. Return each ball to wax paper and repeat process until finished. Allow peanut butter balls to dry on waxed paper before storing in an airtight container.

Peanut Butter Balls ᴷ

1 pound graham crackers, crushed and sifted
1 pound powdered sugar, sifted
1 pound butter, softened
18 ounces peanut butter
1 pound white chocolate bark
1 tablespoon paraffin wax

Crush and sift crackers to powder. Add sifted sugar. Make a well in bowl of this mixture. Add softened butter and peanut butter. Mix together well. In the well or hole, gradually form into the shape of a ball. Chill and roll into balls the size of small walnuts. Chill on wax paper.

Melt chocolate and wax in double boiler over water (water in lower pan and chocolate and wax in top pan). With a toothpick inserted into the middle of a ball, dip the ball into the chocolate. Remove to wax paper. Will harden or dry out. Cool and store in an airtight container until ready to use.

Makes an ample amount. Don't know exactly how many balls it yields but can say that it yields 5 pounds of candy. If there is chocolate left over, put chopped pecans or peanuts into melted chocolate and stir until coated. Spoon mounds onto wax paper for cluster candy.

Buttermilk Caramel Fudge Candy

1 cup buttermilk
1 teaspoon soda
2 cups sugar
3 tablespoons corn syrup
1 teaspoon vanilla flavoring
½ stick butter
1 cup walnuts, chopped (or pecans)
6 quart heavy cooking container

Step 1: In cooking container, combine buttermilk, soda and sugar and stir. Set aside for 5 minutes.

Step 2: Add corn syrup and cook fast, stirring constantly, until mixture is creamy or forms a hard ball when dropped in cold water. Remove from heat. Add flavoring, butter and nuts. Vigorously beat this by hand until well blended. Pour onto a 12 x 8-inch buttered platter. Cool! Cut as desired.

This candy is very rich and has the taste of caramel! For years I made approximately 15 pounds of this at Christmas time. I have also used almond flavoring and pecans instead of the walnuts and vanilla flavoring. This can also be used as a frosting for cakes. Simply delicious!

Awesome Walnut Pralines $\mathcal{K}$

½ pound white sugar
½ pound brown sugar
4 tablespoons hot water
3 cups walnut halves
1 tablespoon butter
1 teaspoon vanilla flavoring

In a saucepan, combine sugars and water. Heat until sugars dissolve. Cook, stirring constantly until firm ball forms when dropped in cold water. Remove from heat. Stir in walnuts, butter and vanilla flavoring. Beat until creamy. Cool until barely warm to the touch. Spoon mounds onto wax paper. Let stand until firm. Wrap individually in cut wax paper and store in a dry place.

Pappy's Peanut Brittle Candy

1 teaspoon vanilla flavoring
1 ½ cups sugar
½ cup white corn syrup
½ cup cold water
1 teaspoon paraffin wax
2 cups raw peanuts
2 teaspoons soda
1 teaspoon salt

In a 6-quart heavy saucepan, bring first 5 ingredients to a boil. Add 2 cups raw peanuts. Cook until peanuts stop popping. Remove from heat! Add soda and salt. Stir or mix well. Pour out onto a 12 x 8-inch greased platter. Cool and break into desired pieces. Store in an airtight container.

When I was growing up, we had get togethers. The neighbors would come to our home. We'd make this recipe and have taffy pullings, ice cream suppers and make popcorn balls, etc. This was before we had electricity, running water, and telephones. We lived in the country and really had a lot of good fellowship.

Tasty Pecan Balls

1 cup butter, softened
½ cup powdered sugar
1 teaspoon vanilla flavoring
2 ¼ cups plain flour
¼ teaspoon salt
1 cup finely chopped walnuts or pecans
Powdered sugar (for outer coat)

In medium mixing bowl, thoroughly mix butter, powdered sugar and vanilla flavoring together. Combine flour, salt and nuts together. Stir flour mixture into butter mixture. Chill dough for 1 hour. Roll into balls the size of walnuts and place onto an ungreased cookie sheet leaving a 1-inch space between balls. Bake at 375 to 400° F until set (10 to 12 minutes). (Do not brown)! Remove from oven and roll in powdered sugar while warm and again when cooled.

Yields approximately 4 dozen pecan balls. Store in airtight container at room temperature when thoroughly cooled until ready to serve. Pecan balls are a big hit for any occasion. Bet ya' can't eat just one.

Monkey Nut Bread

3 large cans small biscuits (10 to a can)
1 cup sugar
3 tablespoons cinnamon
1 cup walnuts, chopped (or pecans)
1 ½ sticks butter, melted
1 teaspoon vanilla flavoring
1 cup light brown sugar, packed

Step 1: Cut each biscuit into 4 pieces with scissors.

Step 2: Mix sugar and cinnamon. Roll biscuit pieces in mixture and arrange in a 10-inch tube pan that has been greased and floured.

Step 3: Sprinkle chopped nuts on top of cut biscuits.

Step 4: Combine melted butter with 1 teaspoon vanilla flavoring and brown sugar. Pour over biscuits and nuts. Bake at 350° F for 30 minutes. Turn out on cake plate and turn upright. Serve warm.

This bread is especially good for party foods as well as other occasions.

Butterscotch Brownies *K*

1 cup sugar
1 stick butter, melted
2 cups graham crackers, finely crushed (powder)
1 cup chopped nuts
2 eggs, beaten
1 teaspoon vanilla flavoring
1 cup butterscotch morsels

Mix sugar and butter. Add remaining ingredients and mix well. Bake in a greased 8-inch square pan at 350° F for 20 minutes (or insert toothpick – should not come out dry). Do not over bake!

Elsie's Nutritional Fruit Bars

1 ½ cups plain flour
1 teaspoon baking powder
¼ teaspoon salt
1 ½ cups fast cooking rolled oats
1 cup brown sugar
¾ cup butter
¾ cup apricot preserves (or strawberry)

Preheat oven to 375° F.

In a medium mixing bowl, sift together flour, baking powder and salt. Stir in the rolled oats and brown sugar. Cut in the butter until crumbly. Pat two-thirds of the crumbly mixture into an 11 x 7 x 1 ½-inch greased baking dish. Spread preserves onto the mixture in the dish. Cover the preserves with remainder of crumbly mixture. Bake for approximately 35 minutes until brown. Cut into bars or squares.

Butterscotch Squares

1/4 cup butter (plus 1 tablespoon)
1 ½ cups graham cracker crumbs
1 cup coconut, frozen flaked
1 cup semi-sweet chocolate morsels
1 cup butterscotch morsels
1 cup walnuts, chopped (or pecans)
15-ounce can sweetened condensed milk

Place butter in a 9-inch square baking pan. Bake at 325° F until melted. Remove from oven. Layer graham cracker crumbs, coconut, chocolate morsels, butterscotch morsels, and nuts in pan with melted butter. (Do not stir.) Spread condensed milk evenly over the top. Bake at 325° F for 30 minutes. Cut into 1 ½-inch squares. Remove to wire racks and allow to cool. These must be thoroughly cooled on both sides. Store in an airtight container. Yields 3 dozen squares. These freeze well.

Brownies ℋ

½ cup butter, plus 2 tablespoons (melted and cooled)
2 eggs, beaten
1 cup sugar
¾ cup plain flour
4 tablespoons cocoa
1/8 teaspoon salt
½ teaspoon baking powder
1 teaspoon vanilla flavoring
1 cup chopped nuts, chopped
Powdered sugar

Melt butter and cool. Blend eggs with sugar. Add cooled butter, flour, cocoa, salt and baking powder. Add vanilla and chopped nuts. Stir 50 times until mixture is uniform. Bake in greased and floured 8-inch square baking pan at 350° F for approximately 30 minutes (or insert toothpick – should not come out dry). Cool before cutting into squares. Dust with powdered sugar or frost with fudge frosting. Do not over bake!

Tracy's Awesome Ice Cream

2 quarts half & half cream
2 14-ounce cans condensed milk
2 teaspoons vanilla flavoring
1-gallon ice cream freezer

In a 3-quart container, combine cream, milk, and flavoring, stirring until mixed. Pour into a 1-gallon ice cream freezer and follow instructions for freezing.

Homemade Ice Cream

For 1 Gallon:

½ cup sugar
6 eggs, beaten
2 cans condensed milk
2 quarts milk
1 tablespoon vanilla flavoring

Takes 25 pounds of ice and 2 boxes of table salt.

In a heavy 6-quart saucepan combine sugar and eggs. Beat until well blended. Add milks. Stir well. While stirring constantly on medium heat, cook until just before the mixture reaches boiling point or coats the back of a spoon. Remove from heat and continue stirring for another minute or two to prevent the custard from scorching. Allow custard to cool! Add flavoring and stir. Pour cooled custard into 1 gallon freezer can (¾ full to allow for expansion during freezing process).

Freezing:

Freeze according to ice cream freezer manual instructions. I use 4 parts of ice to 1 part salt. Layer the ice and salt. Be sure to keep the freezer turning while freezing or the freezer will lock up!

Pappy Murdock's Ice Cream Custard

For 1 ½ gallons:

8 large eggs, beaten
3 ½ cups sugar
1 heaping tablespoon flour
Dash of salt
2 cups half and half
3 quarts milk, plus 1 cup
3 teaspoons vanilla flavoring

In a heavy 6-quart saucepan combine eggs and sugar. Beat with a whisk or hand beaters until well blended. Add flour and salt. Beat until blended. Add half and half and milk to mixture. Stir over medium heat stirring constantly until mixture is about to boil or coats the backside of a spoon. Remove from heat and continue stirring for another minute or two to prevent the custard from scorching. Allow to cool! Add flavoring and freeze according to your hand freezer or electric freezer instructions. Fill freezer ¾ full to allow for expansion.

Our family has enjoyed this delicious ice cream recipe since I was a small child. My father, "Pappy", frequently made this recipe when we had our family get togethers. My homemade chocolate syrup can be used as a topping.

Banana Split or Sundae Topping ᴷ

3 cups sugar
2 1/8 cups water
3 tablespoons corn syrup
1 teaspoon vanilla flavoring
½ cup crushed pineapple
¼ cup Maraschino cherries, chopped
½ cup walnuts, chopped

In a medium saucepan combine sugar, water and corn syrup. Bring to a boil. Boil on medium heat for 10 minutes. Remove from heat and add flavoring, pineapple, cherries and walnuts. Cool and store in refrigerator. Yields 4 cups.

Use for ice cream sundaes, banana splits, ice cream, cake squares, milk shakes, cream cheese pies, pound cake, cheesecake, etc.

Vanilla-Cinnamon-Sugar Sprinkles ᴷ

1 ¾ cups sugar
4 teaspoons cinnamon
5 teaspoons vanilla flavoring

In a one-quart mixing bowl, combine sugar and cinnamon. Mix well. Add vanilla. Toss until well blended. Turn mixture out onto wax paper and allow to dry thoroughly. Break apart the chunks until the mixture is the consistency of sugar. Store in a shaker. Yields about 2 cups.

Sprinkle on pie crust, whipped cream, cinnamon toast, hot or cold chocolate milk, cookies, buttered biscuits, custards, rice pudding, hot oatmeal. For vanilla sugar, omit the cinnamon.

Notes:

Notes:

Look alikes...

Great-grandmother and Great-granddaughter

Susan Caroline "Meek" Herring
23 years old

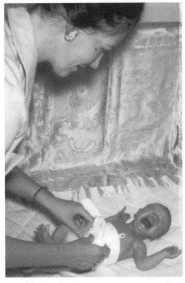

Carolyn "Murdock" Moore
24 years old and
my son Charles, 5 days old
6-19-1963

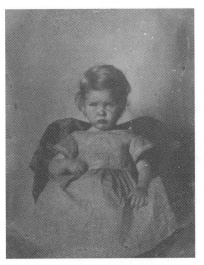

Susan Caroline "Meek" Herring
2 years old

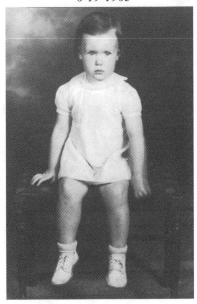

Carolyn "Murdock" Moore
2 years old

In the mid 1990s while cleaning out my mother's closet, I found a box of old pictures. I saw the picture (previous page, upper left) and that it was identical to me. Although I knew the picture *looked* like me, I thought, "I've never worn a high neckline dress." I looked on the back of the picture: "Miss Caroline Meek". This was a picture of my maternal great-grandmother just before she married my great-grandfather Dr. Isaac A. Herring. I was elated to finally know which of my ancestors I really resemble. Among the old photos were other pictures of my maternal great-grandparents Dr. Isaac and Susan Caroline Meek Herring along with his dental certificate.

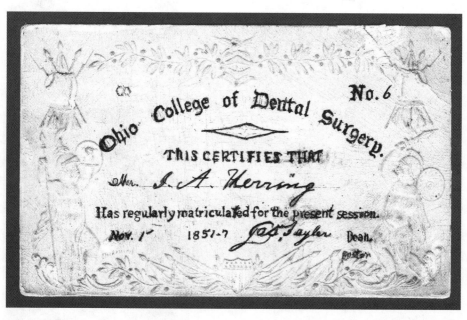

Dr. Isaac A. Herring, D.D.S.

Heavenly Strawberry Pancakes ℋ

1 egg, beaten
1 ¼ cups milk
1 ½ cups self-rising flour
1 teaspoon sugar
1 teaspoon vanilla flavoring
2 tablespoons oil
Dash of salt
Strawberry preserves or fresh crushed strawberries with sugar
Whipped cream

Step 1: In a mixing bowl combine all ingredients except strawberries and whipped cream. Beat until smooth.

Step 2: Using a lightly oiled baker or griddle for frying on medium heat, add about two tablespoonfuls of mixture in the skillet. When bubbles appear in the mixture turn the pancake over to brown on the other side then remove and repeat the process.

Step 3: Stack with 3 teaspoons of crushed fresh strawberries or preserves and top with strawberries and whipped cream. Add strawberry juice on top of whipped topping…. enjoy! Yields six large pancakes.

Substitutions: If using plain flour, add 1 ½ teaspoons baking powder!

Variations: Use ½ cup of mashed bananas in batter or stack with bananas. Use any fruits you desire.

Buttermilk Wheat Pancakes *K*

2 eggs
1 cup milk
1 cup buttermilk
1 cup self-rising flour
1 cup whole wheat flour
2 tablespoons sugar
1 teaspoon baking powder
2 tablespoons corn meal
¼ teaspoon baking soda
¼ teaspoon salt
1 teaspoon vanilla flavoring
4 tablespoons oil

In a large mixing bowl beat eggs. Add milks and beat well. Add rest of ingredients and beat for 1 minute on medium speed.

In an iron baker type skillet on medium heat, pour a small amount of oil making sure oil is evenly distributed over skillet. Pour batter into skillet 5 inches in diameter. When bubbles appear in batter turn the pancake over to brown on the other side. I put a slice of butter on each pancake. Repeat the process until all the batter is used. Yields 12 larges pancakes or 24 medium ones.

Try my syrup on this or your favorite syrup. Batter keeps well for 3 or 4 days in refrigerator. Add milk if mixture is too thick.

Wholesome Silver Dollar Pancakes ℋ

2 eggs
3 cups milk
1/3 cup vegetable oil
1 tablespoon self-rising corn meal
1 cup self-rising four
1 cup whole wheat flour
½ cup rolled oats, quick kind
3 tablespoons baking powder
1 tablespoon sugar
1/8 teaspoon salt
1 teaspoon vanilla flavoring
½ teaspoon cinnamon, ground
Oil for grilling

In a large mixing bowl beat eggs, add milk and beat well. Then add the remaining ingredients and beat for 1 minute. Should be well blended. Ready to make Silver Dollar Pancakes.

In an iron baker skillet or grill on medium heat, pour a small amount of vegetable oil (about a teaspoon). Spoon 1 tablespoon of mixture into separate patty-type rounds. When bubbles appear, flip over and brown opposite side. Add a little butter to top of each pancake, if desired. Remove from heat when brown. Repeat again and again.

I developed this pancake recipe to promote Carolyn's Mapa-Nut. May want to half the recipe! It keeps well refrigerated for 4 days. If mix is too thick add a little milk.

Standard Waffles *K*

1 ¼ cups plain flour
1 ½ teaspoons baking powder
1 teaspoon sugar
½ teaspoon salt
1/3 cup vegetable oil
1 cup milk
2 eggs yolks, beaten
1 teaspoon vanilla flavoring
2 egg whites, beaten stiff

In a large mixing bowl, sift dry ingredients together. Add oil, milk, and egg yolks; beat on medium until blended smooth. Add vanilla flavoring and stir! Fold in stiffly beaten egg whites. Spoon onto preheated waffle iron and allow room for the waffle mix to expand. Yields 6 regular size waffles. Try this with crushed fresh strawberries with whipped cream topping or syrup. Yummy for the tummy—day or night it's out of sight!

You may want to add chopped nuts, fruit, etc. Do not add additional liquid.

Sour Cream Muffins

1 cup self-rising corn meal
½ cup sour cream
2 eggs, beaten
½ cup vegetable oil
1 small can cream-style corn

Mix all together, beating well. Pour into small muffin tins ½ full that have been sprayed with non-stick or hot and greased. Bake at 350° F until done. Broil to a golden brown. Remove from pan and turn upright. We do not cook these very often—they are sinful!

Delicious Harvest Muffins

All ingredients should be room temperature

1 can cherry or apple pie filling
2 cups plain flour
2 teaspoons baking soda
1/8 teaspoon salt
2 eggs, beaten
1 cups sugar
¾ cups oil
2 teaspoons cinnamon
1 teaspoons instant dry coffee
1 cups chopped nuts

In a large mixing bowl, combine all ingredients except nuts. Beat on medium with electric mixer for 2 minutes. Add nuts and stir until well mixed. Spray muffin tins with non-stick cooking spray and fill tins ¾ full of mixture. Bake on 350° F for approximately 12 to 15 minutes or until a toothpick inserted into the middle comes out clean. Remove to wax paper or brown paper bag.

These are great for breakfast or snacks for on the run families. They freeze well. I give these a high rating for taste and texture.

Pappy's Pop Over Biscuits

1 cup self-rising flour
¾ cup milk
1 tablespoon mayonnaise, heaping

Stir ingredients together until smooth. Drop from spoon into hot greased muffin tins ½ full. Bake in 450° F oven 12 to 15 minutes or until brown. Very good!

Country Ham and Red Eye Gravy *K*

2 slices country ham, 1/8 - 1/4 inch thick (approximately 1 ½ pounds)
1/8 cup cold water
1 tablespoon black coffee, optional
10-inch iron skillet, do not grease

Place one ham slice in medium hot skillet and brown on both sides. Remove ham and pour cold water in skillet, should bubble up brown. Pour gravy into a container. Wash skillet and repeat the process. Add coffee if not reddish brown. Yields 8 servings.

True cured country ham should make its own red eye gravy. My mother always put one tablespoon of cream in her gravy, which makes this southern delicacy even more delicious.

Million Dollar MāPa Nut Syrup ᴷ

3 cups sugar
2 1/8 cups water
3 tablespoons corn syrup, white
1 tablespoon vanilla, butter & nut flavoring
¼ teaspoon maple flavoring
½ teaspoon caramel flavoring

In a heavy 4-quart container, combine sugar, water, corn syrup, maple and caramel flavoring. Boil 10 minutes on medium heat. Cool until mixture is lukewarm. Add vanilla, butter, and nut flavoring and mix well. Yields 3 cups. Easily doubled.

I use this syrup in my pecan pies in place of corn syrup.

I developed and manufactured this recipe in the 1980s in Kosciusko, Mississippi, for a craft store that I intended to open. The business was to be called Crafts Unlimited. I named this syrup for my mother and daddy, "Maw and Pa"—my dad made his own brand of maple syrup, which is also in my book. I then changed the name of the syrup to "MāPa Nut". During the developmental stages, the recipe was tested at Mississippi State University while my son was in college there. It ranked in the top five leading brands of pancake syrup when tested by critics at MSU's agriculture panel for shelf life—mold and bacteria count. It was rated "an excellent syrup". I do not use any preservatives. Even today, I have my syrup samples dating back to 1984—and they are still free of spoilage. Many different flavors of syrup can be made from this one basic recipe by changing the flavorings. I'm very proud of this syrup and I hope you'll try it too!

1800's Caramel Syrup (for coloring and flavoring) 𝒦

3 cups sugar
1 ½ cups water

In a large iron skillet, place sugar in skillet on lowest heat setting. Do not stir. It will gradually become a dark golden brown. Add water. Let boil until liquid clears to a brownish color. Cool and store. Will keep a long time in or out of the refrigerator.

I use this in gravies for coloring, syrups, pies, cakes, frostings, etc. Moon shiners use this syrup for flavor as well as coloring when making home-brew whiskey. This caramel syrup has many purposes . . .see if you can find some in my book!

Pappy Murdock's Maple Pancake Syrup

6 cups sugar
4 ¼ cups water
6 tablespoons corn syrup
½ teaspoon maple flavoring

In a heavy saucepan combine all ingredients. Bring to a boil on medium heat and boil for 10 minutes. Cool to lukewarm and pour into sterilized containers. No refrigeration required. Yields 6 cups.

For pancakes, waffles, French toast, etc. For other types of syrups such as strawberry (crushed or sliced), pineapple, cherry, omit maple flavoring and substitute the flavoring you desire. If making a fruit topping, add 1 cup of fruit (drained) after removing syrup from heat. Store in refrigerator. It's very good either way!

Soft Scrambled Eggs ℋ

5 medium eggs
3 tablespoons milk
1 teaspoon butter, melted
Salt and pepper
Medium hot skillet

Combine eggs and milk and beat with a fork for 1 minute. Pour mixtures into medium hot skillet with melted butter. Gently lift cooked egg mixture from bottom of skillet until all is cooked. Do not over cook. Place on plate. Add salt and pepper to taste. Yields 2 servings.

A slice of cheese is great on top of hot eggs.

Roast Beef White Gravy ℋ

4 teaspoons flour, heaping
3 cups beef broth
Salt and pepper to taste

To make thickening, spoon flour into 1-pint jar or 2-cup measuring cup. Add milk to ½ full. Beat until smooth, no lumps (use hand mixer with 1 beater). Add milk to full mark. Blend well.

In a heavy medium saucepan, bring beef broth to a boil. Add thickening to broth and stir constantly until slightly thickened. Add salt and pepper to taste.

This is a five-generation favorite! This recipe should be served over creamed potatoes, oven toast, and pancakes. This may be added to potato soup as a thickener. Usually I leave approximately ¼ cup of chopped roast in my beef broth.

Old Timer's Tomato Gravy ^{K}

3 cups cooked/stewed tomatoes with 2 cups tomato broth
¼ teaspoon salt
2 teaspoons flour, heaping
4 tablespoons sugar or to taste
Milk
¼ teaspoon baking soda
½ stick butter

In a medium saucepan, add salt to stewed tomatoes and broth. Bring to a boil.

In a pint jar, add flour, sugar and milk to fill pint jar to ½ inch of full. Beat with one beater until smooth using an electric mixer. Add soda to tomatoes and then add thickening. Stir until slightly thickened. Remove from heat. Add butter and allow it to melt. Mix well.

This recipe has been passed down through the generations—an all time family favorite. We serve the gravy over split-buttered biscuits. My children love this.

Creamy Grits ^{K}

7 ½ cups cold water
2 cups quick cook grits
¾ teaspoon salt
1 cup milk
1 long spoon for stirring

In a three-quart saucepan with cover, mix water, grits and salt. Bring to a boil. Reduce heat, add cover and simmer for 7 to 10 minutes until thick and done. Add milk and stir. When mixed, pour into eight cereal bowls. Let stand for 3 minutes. Yields 8 cups.

This is my family favorite—I like sweetened grits with butter. So I put ½ stick of butter and ½ cup sugar into the mix just after adding the milk.

Notes:

Notes:

My paternal great aunt...

Mary Murdock
Sept 1, 1841 to Sept 7, 1922

In memory of...

My paternal great-aunt Mary Murdock, daughter of Robert and Elizabeth Richard Murdock. Aunt Mary, born September 1, 1841 in Clinton County, Ohio. She moved to Cedarville, Ohio in 1857 to live with her parents and died September 7, 1922. She is buried in Mossy Creek Cemetery in Cedarville, Ohio.

My father spoke highly of Aunt Mary. He would leave his horse and buggy in her yard while attending school. Aunt Mary's nieces, nephews and neighborhood children used her grounds as a baseball field. She taught them all of the good values of life—an inspiration like no one else.

Aunt Mary never married. She spent her entire life being a missionary of love and charity throughout the branches of our family and others. Aunt Mary touched the lives of so many people throughout her long life until she was thought of as a spiritual factor of her church, community and family. Her labors of love and prayers were greatly felt.

James Howard Murdock, my father, compiled these thoughts concerning Aunt Mary.

The Last of the Big Gardens...

In 1985, my husband, dad, the children and I had a large garden. We canned 165 quarts of green beans, 161 quarts of pickles, relish and pepper sauce, 166 quarts of tomatoes, and 75 jars of jelly. We also blanched and froze 500 ears of corn on the cob and put away 75 quarts of cut and scraped corn. Then there was the 50 quarts of butterbeans, the 48 quarts of peas, the 40 quarts of turnips and mustard greens cooked with salt pork, and the 50 packages of cooked sweet potatoes for pies.

Cultivating, planting, picking, and working a garden is working from can to can't (April to November). By comparison, I have a small garden today. Older and wiser now you might say! I have always kept a log of the amount and particulars of our garden yields.

As an adult, I believe that people should really appreciate good homegrown vegetables—regardless of the work. I highly recommend the practice of growing your own vegetables and I know we've been healthier because of this ritual.

My dad, James Howard Murdock, his sheep and two dogs -- Coco and Tippy Canoe.

Apple Blackberry Jelly *K*

5 cups blackberry juice
5 cups tart apple juice
2 packages powdered pectin
½ teaspoon butter, optional
14 cups sugar
16-quart cooking pot
10-inch large stirring spoon
Long ladle

Place juices into cooking pot. Add pectin and butter, mixing well. On high heat bring mixture to a vigorous, rolling boil that cannot be stirred down. Add sugar and continue stirring, heating mixture again to a rolling boil. Boil hard for 2 minutes. Remove from heat and let stand for 3 minutes. Skim off foam. Pour or ladle jelly immediately into scalded hot jars. Yields 8 pints of jelly.

Adding the butter will reduce the foaming. I test my jelly for thickness by putting a teaspoonful in a saucer and placing the saucer into the freezer for 2 minutes. This jelly has been my favorite for forty years. My mother-in-law served this creamy jelly shortly after my husband and I married. The next time she made it I perched in her kitchen, watching and taking notes. She didn't use pectin and had to use more sugar. I use this jelly recipe for all tart fruit juices. This is delicious on toast, biscuits, pan-cakes, cake layers (while hot) and as a side dish for holidays.

Blanching Fresh Corn for Freezer

Wash and remove silk. In a sixteen-quart container, bring water (enough to cover corn) to boil. Put in as much corn as you can and let corn stay until water is just below boiling point.

Remove with tongs, stacking the corn criss-cross for cooling in a clean tray. When cool near room temperature, let chill in freezer.

Remove from freezer and place corn into large plastic freezer bags leaving enough space at top to tie. Tie each bag of corn and return packages to the freezer.

When cooking blanched corn, remove as much corn as needed for cooking from the freezer bag. This way it conserves space in the freezer. Only add 1 large bag of blanched corn at a time to the freezer to allow corn to freeze properly and not to thaw out your other items in your freezer.

Green Tomato Sandwich Spread

1 quart green tomatoes, ground
1 quart onions, ground
1 quart sweet green and red peppers, ground
½ cup salt
1 quart white vinegar
1 ½ cups sugar
1 quart mayonnaise
9 ounces prepared mustard
Hot green peppers to taste (make into pulp; I use 4 tablespoons)

Mix together tomatoes, onions, peppers and salt. Let stand over night and drain well. Mix vinegar and sugar and add to vegetable mixture. Cook 20 minutes stirring often. Drain well, removing all liquid. Add mayonnaise and mustard and mix well. Put into jars that have been sterilized and prepared for canning. Yields 12 pints.

You can use this for sandwich spread, deviled eggs, tuna salad and potato salad.

Pickled Green Tomatoes ^K

1 gallon green tomatoes, sliced
6 large onions, sliced
½ cup salt (for soaking)
1 tablespoon whole cloves
1 tablespoon whole allspice
1 tablespoon celery seed
1 tablespoon black pepper
3 pods hot peppers, finely chopped
1 tablespoon mustard seed
3 cups vinegar
3 cups sugar

Slice tomatoes and onions. Sprinkle ½ cup salt over them and let stand overnight. Drain well. In a rounded 6-inch cheesecloth add cloves, allspice and celery seed, black pepper, hot peppers, mustard seed and tie securely with a string. Cook spices and vinegar for 10 minutes with the vinegar. Add sugar and tomatoes, cooking for 30 minutes on medium heat, stirring often to prevent burning. Remove spice bag and pack into jars that have been washed, rinsed in hot water and kept hot in oven. Put new caps and tops on and seal tightly. Yields 4 quarts (or 8 pints).

Cold Pack String Beans – Pappy's Way

Caution: Use this method at your own risk. Follow manufacturer's instructions when using pressure cooker for canning or serious injury may result.

Wash, string, and snap string beans or green beans. Pack raw beans into quart jars. Cover with boiling water up to ½ inch from top. Add one teaspoon of salt per quart.

Drop lids into boiled water. Put on jars and tighten with cap. Have 2 to 3 inches of water in pressure cooker bottom. Bring pressure cooker (with lid installed) to a boil, and allow steam to come out of top of pressure cooker for 10 minutes. Then cover steam port with pressure control and allow cooker to pressurize at 10 pounds for 25 minutes. When completed, remove from heat and allow cooker to cool down before removing the pressure control from lid. Once the cooker has cooled, allow pressure (air) to escape for 10 minutes before removing the cooker lid. Tighten jar lids again. Allow canned beans to cool slowly. Caps will pop when sealed. Store in cool, dry place.

Do not allow pressure to fluctuate (go up and down) — keep it on 10 pounds of pressure. This is accomplished by adjusting the heat under the cooker so that the pressure control knob jiggles intermittently.

Lime Cucumber Pickles

Soak cucumbers:

2 cups of pickling lime
2 gallons water
1 gallon cucumbers, sliced ¼-inch crosswise

Mix pickling lime with 2 gallons of water

Soak cucumbers for 24 hours stirring occasionally in lime water. Soak in crockery or enamelware (do not use aluminum ware!). Remove from lime water. Rinse in cool water 3 times.

Soak 3 additional hours in ice and water. Remove carefully when draining or you'll have a lot of broken pickles.

Make syrup:

2 quarts vinegar
8 cups sugar
1 tablespoon salt
Green food coloring
3 tablespoons of pickling spice

Stir all until dissolved. Pour over cucumbers. Let stand 5 or 6 hours or over night. Add 3 tablespoons of pickling spice tied in a white cloth. Boil mixture for 30 minutes. Fill sterilized jars with cucumber slices and pour syrup over cucumbers (leave 1/8-inch space from top of jar). Put caps and tops on and seal jars. Yields 4 quarts of pickles.

If you need more syrup, make up half a batch, boil and finish up.

Pappy's Strawberry Fig Preserves

4 quarts raw figs, cut up
4 6-ounce packages strawberry gelatin
5 pounds sugar

In 8-quart container, add strawberry gelatin and sugar. Mash all ingredients with a potato masher. Bring to a boil and continue to boil for 3 minutes. Put into sterilized jars and seal. Yields 4 quarts, 1 pint.

This same recipe can be used for other fruits such as peaches, pineapple, apricots or pineapple. You will have to adjust your gelatin flavor accordingly for the other fruits.

Miss Bertha's Squash Relish

2 cups ground squash
2 cups ground onion
1 tablespoon salt
½ cup ground sweet bell pepper
1 small pod hot pepper
1 teaspoon turmeric
2 cups white vinegar
2 ½ cups sugar
3 tablespoons pickling spice,
        put in a small thin white cheesecloth and tie off to seal
3-quart saucepan

In saucepan, combine all ingredients and bring to a boil. Reduce heat to medium and cook for 30 minutes. Put in sterilized jars and seal. Yields 4 pints.

Recipe can be used for cucumber relish or can be mixed and used on vegetables or in preparing foods.

Raw Sweet Pepper Relish *K*

19 bell peppers, use 3 or 4 red ones
12 medium white onions
1 stalk celery
1 medium head of cabbage
1 cup salt
1 quart vinegar
1 quart sugar
1 tablespoon white mustard seed

Grind peppers, onions, celery and cabbage in food chopper. Add salt and let it stand over night. Place mixture into a small cheesecloth bag and squeeze out the raw juice. Add remaining ingredients, mixing well. Put into jars and seal. Do not cook. Store in refrigerator. Vinegar and salt are the preservatives for this mixture.

The Hugh M. and Margaret "Starr" Murdock family and children
Mabel Ruth and James Howard, 1908

Notes:

Notes:

My In-laws, the Moore family...

Dutch's mom and dad
Noah Lester and Sadie Ruth "Seago" Moore

Kneeling left to right... Dutch R. Moore, Bath, SC; Melvin L. Moore, Lexington, MS.
Standing left to right... Mrs. Leo "Eloise" Alderman, Lexington, MS; Mrs. Sadie Ruth
Moore (mother), Lexington, MS; Mrs. James "Billie Ruth" Hubbert, Jasper, AL;
Mrs. Nathan "Edith" Aldridge, Lexington, MS; Mrs. James "Loretta" Wilson, San
Jose, CA; Mrs. Jerry "Jean" Marshall, Anderson, IN; Mrs. Louis "Minette" Skinner,
Jackson, MS.

My family or I have used the following remedies when first aid has been required in emergencies. In some cases these home remedies may not have healed the situation but they certainly provided the "victim" with much relief. In no way do I make the claim of a physician, so use these remedies at your own risk.

Apply ice FIRST!
For sprains, any type of insect bites, bruises, broken bones, any type burns, mashed fingers or fever, my mother would always say, "apply ice first." The ice can be applied in several forms and techniques.

Dunking: Pour water over a few cups or ice in a bowl and let the mixture get very cold. Then immerse the injured member of the body.

Ice Pack: Place crushed ice or ice cubes into a bag, add water and tie off. Leave enough air for the bag to be flexible, and then apply to injured area. If you don't have a bag, you can use a white cloth or towel to wrap the ice in to make a compress. I apply this for at least 20 minutes then reapply in a couple of hours. If this doesn't cure or help see a doctor as soon as possible.

For High Fever: I have mixed alcohol with ice water. Apply to the head, neck and rest of the body. Take temperature often to see if you are getting results. If not see a doctor as soon as possible.

Infections: I'm a firm believer in Epsom Salt! Boil 3 cups of water and add 4 tablespoons of Epsom Salt. Stir frequently until the salt dissolves. Immerse infected area for 20 minutes. Repeating 3 times a day is sufficient. This can also be used as a compress by putting 2 tablespoons of Epson Salt in the middle of a white clean cloth. Fold the cloth then dunk into scalding hot water and squeeze out the excess. Apply to the infected area. Repeat 3 times daily.

Note that you should only use a clean white cloth on a wound as colored material can cause additional problems due to the dye in the material.

<u>Stove Burn Infection</u>: Make a loose paste of fresh buttermilk and baking soda. Stir well. Place a generous amount of the paste in a white cloth and fold the cloth. Then apply the cloth to the infected area. Wrap the entire area with plastic wrap and leave on for 12 hours. Reapply one time. This has worked for me many times. I've had some severe burns from removing sweet potato chess pies from the oven. The aloe plant is good for many types of burns. I have squeezed it onto my burns and the burns of my family and friends. It has many uses.

<u>Colds, coughs, allergies, congestion (chest and head)</u>: Make a cough syrup by mixing 1 cup apple cider vinegar with 2 cups non commercial honey (must be produced in your local geographical area) and ½ package peppermint candy sticks. Mix all together by shaking until all is dissolved. Take at least 1 teaspoonful 4 times a day and let it trickle slowly down your throat. I've used this remedy for many years since my body can't tolerate antihistamines.

Note: I now understand that children under the age of 2 years old should not have honey—so adults and older children, this is a great fix!

<u>Preventing Arthritis</u>: Rub turpentine on joints daily (shoulders, hands, knees and feet). My great-grandfather "Poss" Herring lived to be nearly 92 years old and never had arthritis. He contributed the turpentine remedy to his long-lived life free of arthritis.

<u>Arthritic Pain; Muscle soreness due to exertion</u>: Make a rubbing solution by mixing together 16 ounces rubbing alcohol, 4 grated or chopped camphor squares and 24 aspirins in a scalded jar and shake until dissolved. Be sure to label the jar's contents as well as what it is used for. When you have arthritis or muscle soreness, just rub this well into the skin where it hurts. I've applied this rub as many as 4 times daily. Helps a lot! I can't take aspirins due to a stomach condition.

<u>Arthritis Relief</u>: Take 2 soft jels of garlic and parsley four times daily with meals for two weeks then reduce gradually to taking only one gel cap twice a day. I tried this as a suggestion by a family friend when I started having knots developing on the joints in my hands. My hands were very tight and hurting when I woke up each day. Today my hands are free of arthritic pain.

Our bodies are somewhat like a car. If we don't put the right kind of fuel in the car, it doesn't run properly. If we don't eat the proper diet then we can't expect our bodies to function properly. We live in such a fast pace, eat the wrong foods at times and don't get the proper amount of rest each night. I'm really bad about working on borrowed time, promising to pay it back and then I don't do it. After a while it finally catches up with me and then I pay the price. Therefore I take a good vitamin supplement each day.

Vaginal Yeast: In order to keep vaginal yeast under control, I take 1 (250 mg) of vitamin C daily. In the event that I have a flare up, I take 250 mg three times daily until I get the yeast under control, then I reduce it back to the regular dosage of 250 mg daily.

Nail Fungus: At times I work in the dirt without my rubber gloves, which is not good. A fungus developed under three of my nails and they turned black. Medically, I was told to take a prescription that would take six months to take care of the situation. The cost of the medicine was so expensive that I decided to try and see if I could do something about it with home remedy trial and error. Here's what worked for me... I first filed my nails close to the black area. Then I painted my fingernails with diluted name-brand household bleach. Three times a day I did this. It took approximately one month to clear up all of the fungus.

Body Fluid Removal: Using the juice of one fresh lemon in a cup of hot water each morning controls my fluid build up. I call this remedy a lemon toddy for the body! All parts of the lemon are good for a person. We use this when we have a scratchy throat by sucking the lemon then eating the pulp and peeling. Lemons have many uses. They also help to curb the appetite.

Scratchy throat/sore throat: 1 teaspoon of table salt in one glass of rather warm water will help to relieve this condition. Use this as a gargle 3 times a day. This remedy has been around for many generations.

Conjunctivitis of the eyes: I boil one cup of hot water and add ½ teaspoon of table salt. Mix well. Put this mixture in a sterilized eyedropper type bottle. Put two drops into the eye four times a day. I also use this on my dog and cat when their eyes have this condition. This is from the early days.

For sniffles/sinus: I boil one pint of water for one minute. Cool! Dissolve 1 teaspoon of table salt into the cooled water. Pour a small amount of salted water in the palm of your hand. Sniff the solution into only one nostril at a time, blocking off the other nostril by pressing with the index finger. Repeat twice daily.

Wart Removal: Soak a cotton swab in apple cider vinegar. Apply on the wart for several minutes letting it dry each time applied. Cover with a band-aid. Repeat three times daily until wart disappears.

Hiccup Cure: Put 1 teaspoon of granulated sugar on your tongue and let it dissolve slowly followed by an eight-ounce glass of water. Another cure is to sip 1 tablespoon of dill pickle juice. Another one is to take about 1/8 cup of water, strike an old fashioned match, blow out match and dunk into the water while the match is smoking, remove the match and drink the water.

Poison ivy/poison oak rash: Make a paste of water and uncooked oatmeal and apply to the infected area. Wrap with a white sterilized cloth. Leave on for several hours and then wash off the oatmeal. Reapply.

Baby Colic/Cramps: Bring to boil 2 ounces of water. Add ½ teaspoon sugar. Stir until dissolved. Cool until lukewarm. Add 5 drops of whiskey. Stir well. Pour into baby's bottle and feed. This remedy allows the baby to expel the gas. Dolph Hammett of Lexington, Mississippi, a father of thirteen children gave my husband this remedy. I told Dr. Brumby what I'd done. He said, "It's as good as you can get for colic." What a relief! I thought the doctor was going to scold me. This really works.

Sugar Diabetes: This is an old Indian remedy. Eat ground cinnamon. It helps to balance the sugar in the blood and keep the sugar at a good level. I eat cinnamon on toast, eggs, pudding or right out of a spoon. I eat at least ¼ teaspoonful at a time ~~four times~~ a day. *once daily* --

Nausea: Put ½ teaspoon of ground ginger in an eight-ounce glass of water, mix well and drink.

Minor Indigestion: Mix ¼ teaspoon of baking soda in six ounces of water and drink.

Fire Ant Bites: Apply apple cider vinegar to reduce the sting. One application is usually all that it takes. This works for me!

Yellow Jacket Stings: Apply household ammonia on the area.

Muscle Fatigue: Massage with rubbing alcohol. This is very refreshing.

Brown Recluse Spider Bite: In 1994 I was bitten by a brown recluse spider. This caused a very painful and burning sensation at the same time. I tried using my other home remedies such as apple cider vinegar, name brand household bleach, baking soda and household ammonia. None of these remedies helped. In two hours, I had a ¼ inch swelling on the upper part of my stomach that was 5 inches in diameter. Nine hours after being bitten the pain was unbearable. I mixed buttermilk and baking soda and put it into a handkerchief. I placed this on the raised area and sealed it with plastic wrap. An hour later the pain was gone and I went to bed. I reapplied this mixture five times the following day. The pain was gone and the swelling and redness was reduced. My son and I were taking line dancing classes that night and there were three Registered Nurses there. One of them asked to look at my stomach. They wanted me to go to the hospital immediately to get help for the bite. After they told me about the damage that a brown recluse spider could cause I called my doctor and asked what did I do wrong. He said I should have applied ice first. He said to apply cortisone cream several times a day, which I did. Today, all I have to remind me of the bite is a white scar the size of a match head. I am very fortunate. Today, I still use the buttermilk and soda remedy as a result of my experience—and I'll never forget to use ice first.

Notes:

Notes:

Notes:

"K" Carolyn and Dutch

SCHOOL DAYS 1949-50
KOSCIUSKO

School Days
1946-47

"The Hills and Valleys of West Virginia"

My Great Aunt Sarah Starr of Harrisville
and Indian Creek, West Virginia painted
this beautiful picture on the back of glass.
She was one gifted lady.

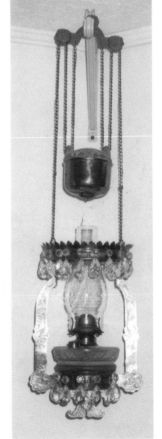

The adjustable lamp was my favorite lamp to
study by before we had electricity. They hang
this way in my living room.

Mabel Ruth and James Howard Murdock, my father, children of:
The Hugh McMillian Murdock's, Cedarville, Ohio

My father, James Howard Murdock
1913, age 16, Cedarville, Ohio
His double barrel shotgun

Cousins, Fred and Jeannie Starr
Harrisville, West Virginia

Maternal Aunt Carrie and
Oakley McClellan
Biloxi, Mississippi

Murdock Family
Left to right, Margaret, dad, mother, Hugh, Elsie and Carolyn
1949, Kosciusko, Mississippi

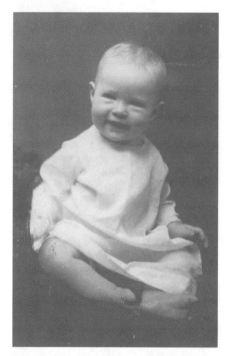

My sister Elsie, 1928

My brother Hugh, 1933

The first car that I remember our family having.

1917 Mabel Ruth Murdock, my paternal aunt (right) and friends riding in my grandfathers sled. Cedarville, Ohio had continuous snow from November to February.

Mabel Ruth Murdock, my paternal aunt (center) with friends taking a ride in my grandfathers horse and buggy.
"This looks like fun to me"

My husband, Dutch

My son, Charles, 2 years old

*My brother,
Hugh*

School Days
1942-43

*The Starr connection Aunt Sarah and family
Harrisville, West Virginia*

My maternal grandparents, Ike and Minnie

*My brother,
Hugh*

School Days
1945-46

In memory of Florence Price...

After the rest of my family either married or returned to Mississippi, I lived in Springfield, South Carolina with my brother Hugh. Hugh worked shifts at the Savannah River Plant. I could not stand the thoughts of staying alone at night. While Hugh worked night shifts Florence Price stayed with me.

In August 1957, Florence cried when she learned we were moving back to Mississippi. My brother Hugh asked her why she was crying. She said that we were the only family she had ever known. Hugh asked her if she wanted to move with us to Mississippi. She was elated. She packed her clothes and we were soon on our journey. Hugh drove his 1931 Ford A-Model convertible with a boxer dog named Linda and her four puppies. I drove his 1957 yellow Ford Fairlane and pulling a trailer. Twenty-four hours later we pulled into the driveway of the Murdock family home place.

Florence was a jolly lady who loved us as we loved her. She loved to sing and we often harmonized together. She made many friends around our community. I have many good memories of things we did together.

Florence was born and grew up around St. Johns Island near Charleston, South Carolina. She gave birth to six children who were later taken away from her. She never told us why. Florence died in 1974 at approximately 90 years old and is buried in Buffalo United Methodist Church Cemetery on Oprah Winfrey Drive in Kosciusko, Mississippi. Florence was a regular part of our family life for about twenty-one years. Her picture is in the family photos section.

Index